Susan Ge

Praise for

CLOSE TO THE MACHINE

"This book is a little masterpiece, an exquisitely melancholy cry from a body disappearing into the machine. It is a wrenching swan-song for human beings. I have never read anything like it because nothing like it could have been written before. Here is the perfect way to say good-bye to the millennium."

—Andrei Codrescu

"Computer programmers are remaking the world. Here is ground truth about that world-making and brilliant insider critique of it. The reader vibrates between delight and alarm on every page. It's wonderful to see such a blending of code craft and word craft (and no small measure of life craft) in the author. It's a perfect book for City Lights— longstanding purveyor of subversive honesty and art."

—Stewart Brand

"Ullman's work has the keenness of all my favorite writing. . . . Here, her talent enables readers to explore intimately, and without forced profundity, one of the biggest questions of our time: What is it about the numerical, seemingly inhuman world of computing that holds such powerful, wholly human allure."

—Brad Wieners, editor, Wired Books

"Ullman's story of life in the electronic world is a reckoning, a warning, a seduction. It is also very funny."

—Rebecca Brown

"There are no crazed hackers here; no zen-master software moguls; no media stereotypes; just a wonderfully written book about Ullman's days and nights at the heart of the new machine. I recommend it with unfettered enthusiasm."

—Jon Carroll, *San Francisco Chronicle*

"Ullman wittily spills the beans about the technology on which we all depend."

—*Publishers Weekly*

"Ellen Ullman, a software engineer, writes with the energy of Boswell, the clarity of Orwell, and the warmth of Montaigne. You may wonder: how could a software engineer write so well? Ullman is a wonderful writer, and *Close to the Machine* is a wonderful book."

—John Gehl, editor, *Educom Review*

"*Close to the Machine* so very accurately paints the never ending race a programmer must run to make these (damn) wonderful computers useful to humanity. I found myself nodding in violent agreement at her concise summaries of programming hell."

—Dan Lynch, chairman, Cybercash

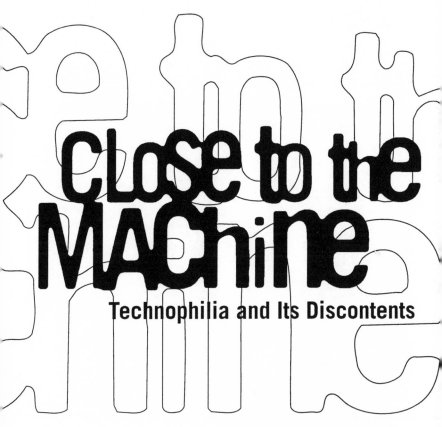

Close to the MAChine

Technophilia and Its Discontents

Ellen Ullman

City Lights Books
San Francisco

Cover design: Rex Ray
Book design: Nancy J. Peters
Typography: Harvest Graphics

Cataloging-in-Publication Data

Ullman, Ellen.
    Close to the machine : technophilia and its discontents / by
Ellen Ullman.
        p.   cm.
    ISBN: 0-87286-337-9 (cl).— ISBN 0-87286-332-8 (pb)
    1. Ullman, Ellen. 2. Computer programmers — Biography.
I. Title.
QA76.2.U43A3   1997
005.1'092 — dc21
[B]   97-27244
                                                        CIP

City Lights Books are available to bookstores through our primary
distributor: Subterranean Company, P.O. Box 160, 265 S. 5th St.,
Monroe, OR 97456. 541-847-5274. Toll-free orders 800-274-7826.
FAX 541-847-6018. Our books are also available through library
jobbers and regional distributors. For personal orders and catalogs,
please write to City Lights Books, 261 Columbus Avenue,
San Francisco, CA 94133.

CITY LIGHTS BOOKS are edited by Lawrence Ferlinghetti and
Nancy J. Peters and published at the City Lights Bookstore,
261 Columbus Avenue, San Francisco, CA 94133.

Acknowledgments

With unending gratitude for the help of Clara Basile,
Naomi Epel, and Jeanette Gurevitch.

Three short sections of this book, in a slightly different form, were first presented as the commentaries "On Becoming an Old Programmer," "My Virtual Company," and "In Their Fifties" on the National Public Radio program "All Things Considered."

For Nancy

To my father

Contents

[0] Space Is Numeric   1

[1] Transactions   17

[2] Sushi   39

[3] Real Estate   53

[4] Software and Suburbia   65

[5] New, Old, and Middle Age   95

[6] Virtuality   123

[7] Money   149

[8] The Passionate Engineer   175

[9] Driving   185

[0]

I HAVE NO IDEA WHAT TIME IT IS. There are no windows in this office and no clock, only the blinking red LED display of a microwave, which flashes 12:00, 12:00, 12:00, 12:00. Joel and I have been programming for days. We have a bug, a stubborn demon of a bug. So the red pulse no-time feels right, like a read-out of our brains, which have somehow synchronized themselves at the same blink rate.

"But what if they select all the text and—"

"—hit Delete."

"Damn! The NULL case!"

"And if not we're out of the text field and they hit space—"

"—yeah, like for—"

"—no parameter—"

"Hell!"

"So what if we space-pad?"

"I don't know. . . . Wait a minute!"

"Yeah, we could space-pad—"

"—and do space as numeric."

"Yes! We'll call SendKey(space) to—?

"—the numeric object."

"My God! That fixes it!"

"Yeah! That'll work if—"

"—space is numeric!"

"—if space is numeric!"

We lock eyes. We barely breathe. For a slim moment, we are together in a universe where two human beings can simultaneously understand the statement "if space is numeric!"

Joel and I started this round of debugging on Friday morning. Sometime later, maybe Friday night, another programmer, Danny, came to work. I suppose it must be Sunday by now because it's been a while since we've seen my client's employees around the office. Along the way, at odd times of day or night that have completely escaped us, we've ordered in three meals of Chinese food, eaten six large pizzas, consumed several beers, had innumerable bottles of fizzy water, and finished two entire bottles of wine. It has occurred to me that if people really knew how software got written, I'm not sure if they'd give their money to a bank or get on an airplane ever again.

What are we working on? An artificial intelligence project to find "subversive" talk over international phone lines? Software for the second start-up of a Silicon Valley executive banished from his first company? A system to help AIDS patients get services across a city? The details escape me just now. We may be helping poor sick people or tuning a set of low-level routines to verify bits on a distributed database protocol—I don't care. I should care; in another part of my being—later, perhaps when we emerge from this room full of computers—I will care very much why and for whom and for what purpose I am writing software. But just now: no. I have passed through a membrane where the real world and its uses no longer matter. I am a software engineer, an independent contractor working for a department of a city government. I've hired Joel and three other programmers to work with me. Down the hall is Danny, a slim guy in wire-rimmed glasses who comes to work with a big, wire-haired dog. Across the bay in his converted backyard shed is Mark, who works on the database. Somewhere, probably asleep by now, is Bill the network guy. Right now, there are only two things in the universe that matter to us. One, we have some bad bugs to fix. Two, we're supposed to install the system on Monday, which I think is tomorrow.

"Oh, no, no!" moans Joel, who is slumped over his keyboard. "No-*o-o-o*." It comes out in a long wail. It has the sound of lost love, lifetime regret. We've both been programmers long enough to know that we are at *that place*. If we find one more serious problem we can't solve right away, we will not make it. We won't install. We'll go the terrible, familiar way of all software: we'll be late.

"No, no, no, no. What if the members of the set start with spaces. Oh, God. It won't work."

He is as near to naked despair as has ever been shown to me by anyone not in a film. Here, in *that place,*

3

we have no shame. He has seen me sleeping on the floor, drooling. We have both seen Danny's puffy white midsection — young as he is, it's a pity — when he stripped to his underwear in the heat of the machine room. I have seen Joel's dandruff, light coating of cat fur on his clothes, noticed things about his body I should not. And I'm sure he's seen my sticky hair, noticed how dull I look without make-up, caught sight of other details too intimate to mention. Still, none of this matters anymore. Our bodies were abandoned long ago, reduced to hunger and sleeplessness and the ravages of sitting for hours at a keyboard and a mouse. Our physical selves have been battered away. Now we know each other in one way and one way only: the code.

Besides, I know I can now give him pleasure of an order which is rare in any life: I am about to save him from despair.

"No problem," I say evenly. I put my hand on his shoulder, intending a gesture of reassurance. "The parameters *never* start with a space."

It is just as I hoped. His despair vanishes. He becomes electric, turns to the keyboard and begins to type at a rapid speed. Now he is gone from me. He is disappearing into the code — now that he knows it will work, now that I have reassured him that, in our universe, the one we created together, space can indeed be forever and reliably numeric.

The connection, the shared thought-stream, is cut. It has all the frustration of being abandoned by a lover just before climax. I know this is not physical love. He is too young, he works for me; he's a man and I've been tending toward women; in any case, he's too prim and business-schooled for my tastes. I know this sensation is not *real* attraction: it is only the spillover, the excess charge, of the mind back into the abandoned body. *Only.* Ha. This is another real-world thing that does not matter. My entire self wants to melt into this brilliant, electric being who has shared his mind with me for twenty seconds.

Restless, I go into the next room where Danny is slouched at his keyboard. The big, wire-haired dog growls at me. Danny looks up, scowls like his dog, then goes back to typing. I am the designer of this system, his boss on this project. But he's not even trying to hide his contempt. Normal programmer, I think. He has fifteen windows full of code open on his desktop. He has overpopulated his eyes, thoughts, imagination. He is drowning in bugs and I know I could help him, but he wants me dead just at the moment. I am the last-straw irritant. *Talking:* Shit! What the hell is wrong with me? Why would I want to *talk* to him? Can't I see that his stack is overflowing?

"Joel may have the overlapping controls working," I say.

"Oh, yeah?" He doesn't look up.

"He's been using me as a programming dummy," I say. "Do you want to talk me through the navigation errors?" Navigation errors: bad. You click to go some-where but get somewhere else. Very, very bad.

"What?" He pretends not to hear me.

"Navigation errors. How are they?"

"I'm working on them." Huge, hateful scowl. Contempt that one human being should not express to another under any circumstances. Hostility that should kill me, if I were not used to it, familiar with it, practiced in receiving it. Besides, we are at *that place*. I know that this hateful programmer is all I have between me and the navigation bug. "I'll come back later," I say.

Later: how much later can it get? Daylight can't be far off now. This small shoal of pre-installation madness is washing away even as I wander back down the hall to Joel.

"Yes! It's working!" says Joel, hearing my approach.

He looks up at me. "You were right," he says. The ultimate one programmer can say to another, the accolade given so rarely as to be almost unknown in our species. He looks right at me as he says it: "You were right. As always."

This is beyond rare. *Right:* the thing a programmer desires above, beyond all. *As always:* unspeakable, incalculable gift.

"I could not have been right without you," I say. This is true beyond question. "I only opened the door. You figured out how to go through."

I immediately see a certain perfume advertisement: a man holding a violin embraces a woman at a piano. I want to be that ad. I want efficacies of reality to vanish, and I want to be the man with violin, my programmer to be the woman at the piano. As in the ad, I want the teacher to interrupt the lesson and embrace the student. I want the rules to be broken. Tabu. That is the name of the perfume. I want to do what is taboo. I am the boss, the senior, the employer, the person in charge. So I must not touch him. It is all taboo. Still—

Danny appears in the doorway.

"The navigation bug is fixed. I'm going home."

"I'll test it—"

"It's fixed."

He leaves.

It is sometime in the early morning. Joel and I are not sure if the night guard is still on duty. If we leave, we may not get back up the elevator. We leave anyway.

We find ourselves on the street in a light drizzle. He has on a raincoat, one that he usually wears over his too-prim, too-straight, good-biz-school suits. I have on a second-hand-store leather bomber jacket, black beret, boots. Someone walking by might wonder what we were doing together at this still-dark hour of the morning.

"Goodnight," I say. We're still charged with thought energy. I don't dare extend my hand to shake his.

"Goodnight, " he says.

We stand awkwardly for two beats more. "This will sound strange," he says, "but I hope I don't see you tomorrow."

We stare at each other, still drifting in the wake of our shared mind-stream. I know exactly what he means. We will only see each other tomorrow if I find a really bad bug.

"Not strange at all," I say, "I hope I don't see you, either."

I don't see him. The next day, I find a few minor bugs, fix them, and decide the software is good enough. Mind-meld fantasies recede as the system goes live. We install the beginnings of a city-wide registration system for AIDS patients. Instead of carrying around soiled and wrinkled eligibility documents, AIDS clients only have to prove once that they are really sick and really poor. It is an odd system, if I think of it, certifying that people are truly desperate in the face of possible death.

Still, this time I'm working on a "good" project, I tell myself. We are *helping* people, say the programmers over and over, nearly in disbelief at their good fortune. Three programmers, the network guy, me—fifty-eight years of collective technical experience—and the idea of helping people with a computer is a first for any of us.

Yet I am continually anxious. How do we protect this database full of the names of people with AIDS? Is a million-dollar computer system the best use of continually shrinking funds? It was easier when I didn't have to think about the real-world effect of my work. It was easier— and I got paid more—when I was writing an "abstracted interface to any arbitrary input device." When I was designing a "user interface paradigm," defining a "test-bed methodology." I could disappear into weird passions of logic. I could stay in a world peopled entirely by pro- grammers, other weird logic-dreamers like myself, all caught up in our own inner electricities. It was easier and more valued. In my profession, software engineering, there is something almost shameful in this helpful, social-services system we're building. The whole project smacks of "end users"—those contemptible, oblivious people who just want to use the stuff we write and don't care how we did it.

"What are you working on?" asked an acquaintance I ran into at a book signing. She's a woman with her own start-up company. Her offices used to be in the loft just below mine, two blocks from South Park, in San Francisco's Multimedia Gulch. She is tall and strikingly attractive; she wears hip, fashionable clothes; her company already has its first million in venture-capital funding. "What are you working on," she wanted to know, "I mean, that isn't under non-D?"

Under non-D. Nondisclosure. That's the cool thing to be doing: working on a system so new, so just started-up, that you can't talk about it under pain of lawsuit.

"Oh, not much," I answered, trying to sound breezy. A city-wide network for AIDS service providers: how unhip could I get? If I wanted to do something for people with AIDS, I should make my first ten million in stock options, then attend some fancy party where I wear a red ribbon on my chest. I should be a sponsor for Digital Queers. But actually working on a project for end users? Where my client is a government agency? In the libertarian world of computing, where "creating wealth" is all, I am worse than uncool: I am aiding and abetting the bureaucracy, I am a net consumer of federal taxes—I'm what's wrong with this country.

"Oh, I'm basically just plugging in other people's

software these days. Not much engineering. You know," I waved vaguely, "*plumbing* mostly."

My vagueness paid off. The woman winked at me. "Networks," she said.

"Yeah. Something like that," I said. I was disgusted with myself, but, when she walked away, I was relieved.

The end users I was so ashamed of came late in the system development process. I didn't meet them until the software was half-written. This is not how these things are supposed to go—the system is not supposed to predate the people who will use it—but it often goes that way anyhow.

The project was eight months old when my client-contact, a project manager in a city department, a busi-ness-like woman of fifty, finally set up a meeting. Representatives of several social-service agencies were invited; eight came. A printed agenda was handed around the conference table. The first item was "Review agenda." My programmer-mind whirred at the implication of end-less reiteration: Agenda. Review agenda. Agenda. Forever.

"Who dreamed up this stuff?" asked a woman who directed a hospice and home-care agency. "This is all use-less!" We had finally come to item four on the agenda: "Review System Specifications." The hospice director waved a big stack of paper—the specifications arrived at by a "task force"—then tossed it across the table. A heavy-set woman apparently of Middle-Eastern descent, she had probably smoked a very large number of cigarettes in the course of her fifty-odd years on earth. Her laugh trailed off into a chesty rumble, which she used as a kind of drum roll to finish off her scorn.

The other users were no more impressed. A black woman who ran a shelter—elegant, trailing Kente cloth. She arranged her acres of fabric as some sort of displacement for her boredom; each time I started talking, I seemed to have to speak over a high jangle of her many bracelets set to play as she, ignoring me with something that was not quite hostility, arranged and rearranged herself. A woman who ran a clinic for lesbians, a self-described "femme" with hennaed hair and red fingernails: "Why didn't someone come talk to us first?" she asked. A good question. My client sat shamefaced. A young, handsome black man, assistant to the hospice director, quick and smart: he simply shook his head and kept a skeptical smile on his face. Finally a dentist and a doctor, two white males who looked pale and watery in this sea of diversity: they worried that the system would get in the way of giving services. And around the table they went, complaint by complaint.

I started to panic. Before this meeting, the users existed only in my mind, projections, all mine. They were abstractions, the initiators of tasks that set off remote procedure calls; triggers to a set of logical and machine events that ended in an update to a relational database on a central server. Now I was confronted with their fleshly existence. And now I had to think about the actual existence of the people who used the services delivered by the users' agencies, sick people who were no fools, who would do what they needed to do to get pills, food vouchers, a place to sleep.

I wished, earnestly, I could just replace the abstractions with the actual people. But it was already too late for that. The system pre-existed the people. Screens were prototyped. Data elements were defined. The machine events already had more reality, had been with me longer, than the human beings at the conference table. Immediately, I saw it was a problem not of replacing one reality with another but of two realities. I was there at the edge: the interface of the system, in all its existence, to the people, in all their existence.

I talked, asked questions, but I saw I was operating at a different speed from the people at the table. Notch down, I told myself. *Notch down.* The users were bright, all too sensitive to each other's feelings. Anyone who was the slightest bit cut off was gotten back to sweetly: "You were saying?" Their courtesy was structural, built into their "process." I had to keep my hand over my mouth to keep from jumping in. Notch down, I told myself again. *Slow down.* But it was not working. My brain whirred out a stream of logic-speak: "The agency sees the client records if and only if there is a relationship defined between the agency and the client," I heard myself saying. "By definition, as soon as the client receives services from the agency, the system considers the client to have a relationship with the provider. An internal index is created which represents the relationship." The hospice director closed her eyes to concentrate. She would have smoked if she could have; she looked at me as if through something she had just exhaled.

I took notes, pages of revisions that had to be done immediately or else doom the system to instant disuse. The system had no life without the user, I saw. I'd like to say that I was instantly converted to the notion of real human need, to the impact I would have on the working lives of these people at the table, on the people living with AIDS; I'd like to claim a sudden sense of real-world responsibility. But that would be lying. What I really thought was this: I must save the system.

I ran off to call the programmers. Living in my hugely different world from the sick patients, the forbearing service providers, the earnest and caring users at the meeting, I didn't wait to find a regular phone. I went into the next room, took out my cell phone, began punching numbers into it, and hit the "send" button: "We have to talk," I said.

By the time I saw Joel, Danny, and Mark, I had reduced the users' objections to a set of five system changes. I would like to use the word "reduce" like a cook: something boiled down to its essence. But I was aware that the real human essence was already absent from the list I'd prepared. An item like "How will we know if the clients have TB?"—the fear of sitting in a small, poorly ventilated room with someone who has medication-resistant TB, the normal and complicated biological urgency of that question—became a list of data elements to be added to the screens and the database. I tried to communicate some of the sense of the meeting to the programmers. They were interested, but in a mild, backgrounded way. Immediately, they seized the list of changes and, as I watched, they turned them into further abstractions.

"We can add a parameter to the remote procedure call."

"We should check the referential integrity on that."

"Should the code be attached to that control or should it be in global scope?"

"Global, because this other object here needs to know about the condition."

"No! No globals. We agreed. No more globals!"

We have entered the code zone. Here thought is telegraphic and exquisitely precise. I feel no need to slow myself down. On the contrary, the faster the better. Joel runs off a stream of detail, and halfway through a sentence, Mark, the database programmer, completes the thought. I mention a screen element, and Danny, who programs the desktop software, thinks of two elements I've forgotten. Mark will later say all bugs are Danny's fault, but, for now, they work together like cheerful little parallel-processing machines, breaking the problem into pieces that they attack simultaneously. Danny will later become the angry programmer scowling at me from behind his broken code, but now he is still a jovial guy with wire-rimmed glasses and a dog that accompanies him everywhere. "Neato," he says to something Mark has proposed, grinning, patting the dog, happy as a clam.

"Should we modify the call to AddUser—"

"—to check for UserType—"

"Or should we add a new procedure call—"

"—something like ModifyPermissions."

"But won't that add a new set of data elements that repeat—"

"Yeah, a repeating set—"

"—which we'll have to—"

"—renormalize!"

Procedure calls. Relational database normalization. Objects going in and out of scope. Though my mind is racing, I feel calm. It's the spacey calm of satellites speeding over the earth at a thousand miles per second: relative to each other, we float. The images of patients with AIDS recede, the beleaguered service providers are forgotten, the whole grim reality of the epidemic fades. We give ourselves over to the sheer fun of the technical, to the nearly sexual pleasure of the clicking thought-stream.

Some part of me mourns, but I know there is no other way: human needs must cross the line into code. They must pass through this semipermeable membrane where urgency, fear, and hope are filtered out, and only reason travels across. There is no other way. Real, death-inducing viruses do not travel here. Actual human confusions cannot live here. Everything we want accomplished, everything the system is to provide, must be denatured in its crossing to the machine, or else the system will die.

[1]

"SOFTWARE IS TEAMWORK," SAID THE WOMAN IN THE beautiful black outfit. The pants were wide-legged and had a lacy, vaguely see-through surface; the jacket was of wool that draped like silk. In her hand was a glass of twelve-year-old Bordeaux. We were at a wine-tasting party. "Systems analysts, user representatives, department managers, programming managers, programmers, testers" — the woman's wine glass moved slowly left to right — "an organized team of players working in cooperation to meet well-defined objectives."

I thought about Danny and Mark and Joel. Somehow I couldn't see them in this well-run team of players. But the woman was a vice president at a very large credit-card corporation. She got paid to talk this way. "Corporate users," I thought. They live where software edges into business. Corporate end users: wildebeests of the programming food chain, consumers, roaming perilously far from the machine.

I realized I was thinking this because I was practically an end user myself, working on the AIDS project, and I had a deep need to distance myself from anything remotely resembling corporate systems. I'm a software engineer, I kept telling myself, an *engineer.* I had spent too long at this—nineteen years—to give up my technical credentials just yet.

But beyond any techno-ego considerations, I was simply terrified of this woman. She reminded me of everything I'm not: WASP, pleasant in social situations, effective at corporate meetings. Next to her, I felt hopelessly Jewish, obsessed, driven. A woman like this would never display obsession, would never panic the first time she met her end users across a conference table. I used to be amazed at high-level corporate managers and officers. I wondered, "How do they suppress their complications, doubts, and worries? How do they present this mild, certain, straightforward demeanor?" After many years, I understood there was no suppression to it: they really were people without many complications.

The vice president went on to describe her development process. "Everything we do starts from a complete requirements analysis."

I imagined months, years of meetings; reams of paper. Flowcharts. Spreadsheets.

"Then it moves to the systems analysts, who turn those requirements into system objectives and timelines."

More meetings, documents, flowcharts, spreadsheets. Dataset listings. Equipment requirements. Proposed configuration drawings.

"User departments then review the system functional specification."

Contentious meetings. Users trying to articulate needs that don't fit neatly into all the flowcharts and drawings. Compromises. Promises of "future development" to take unaddressed needs into account.

"Then it moves to programming," said the vice president.

She swirled the glass, inhaled the nose, took a sip of the Bordeaux. "For us, programming is the smallest part of the process. Lovely wine," she said. I nodded vague agreement out of courtesy. The vice president and I at least shared a taste for red wine and a fondness for wearing all black. "Since we go through all the right steps, eighty to ninety percent of the systems we specify go on to successful deployment."

She was triumphant. She drained her glass.

Still, I thought of the place where "it moves to programming." I asked and found out that the vice president didn't see much of the programmers; they were levels beneath her; they worked in a building a ten-minute drive from her office. When "it moved to programming," it literally moved, far away from her, into some realm where other managers had to deal with the special species of human being known as programmers. I noticed how, perhaps unconsciously, the movement to programming was where the vice president stopped to drink the wine. I noticed how quickly she moved from programming to "deployment"—there, done, success. In that place she ran over so quickly was a dimly understood process: programmers turning the many pages of specifications into a foreign language called code.

"If managing programmers were so easy, there wouldn't be so many books on the subject," I said, trying not to sound defensive.

"Uhmm," she demurred. "Quite possibly."

Here I was on more certain ground. I knew no one can manage programmers. "A project leader I know once said that managing programmers is like trying to herd cats."

"Uhmm," she demurred again. "Clever."

"I mean, you don't want them to stop being cats," I kept on bravely. "You don't want obedient dogs. You want all that weird strangeness that makes a good programmer. On the other hand, you do have to get them somehow moving in the same direction."

"Clever," she murmured again, her focus beginning to roam around the room.

There it was: the thing that makes me so afraid of high-level managers. That impenetrable surface, the apparent lack of complication, doubt, even curiosity. Was she covering discomfort, ignorance, fear of appearing ignorant? Or was she simply bored by me? There was no way I could know. Extrapolating from myself, I thought: What a marvelous ability to affect self-assurance! What superb management of professionally undesirable traits! I longed for such ability to hide my feelings. I imagined someday I would sit in a meeting and be transparent as water, quietly emanating authority.

Then I remembered that she probably had no fears or doubts around me. All she knew about me is what I'd told her: that I'm a software engineer. I'm no one.

I thought of her programmers sitting in their cubicles, surrounded by the well-dressed swirl of analysts and managers. The "system" comes to them done on paper, in English. "All" they have to do is write the code. But somewhere in that translation between the paper and the code, the clarity breaks down. The world as humans understand it and the world as it must be explained to computers come together in the programmer in a strange state of disjunction.

The project begins in the programmer's mind with the beauty of a crystal. I remember the feel of a system at the early stages of programming, when the knowledge I am to represent in code seems lovely in its structuredness. For a time, the world is a calm, mathematical place. Human and machine seem attuned to a cut-diamond-like state of grace. Once in my life I tried methamphetamine: that speed high is the only state that approximates the feel of a project at its inception. Yes, I understand. Yes, it can be done. Yes, how straightforward. Oh yes. I *see*.

Then something happens. As the months of coding go on, the irregularities of human thinking start to emerge. You write some code, and suddenly there are dark, unspecified areas. All the pages of careful documents, and still, between the sentences, something is missing.

Human thinking can skip over a great deal, leap over small misunderstandings, can contain ifs and buts in untroubled corners of the mind. But the machine has no corners. Despite all the attempts to see the computer as a brain, the machine has no foreground or background. It cannot simultaneously do something and withhold for later something that remains unknown.* In the painstaking working out of the specification, line by code line, the programmer confronts all the hidden workings of human thinking.

Now begins a process of frustration. The programmer goes back to the analysts with questions, the analysts to the users, the users to their managers, the managers back to the analysts, the analysts to the programmers. It turns out that some things are just not understood. No one knows the answers to some questions. Or worse, there are too many answers. A long list of exceptional situations is revealed, things that occur very rarely but that occur all the same. Should these be programmed? Yes, of course. How else will the system do the work human beings need to accomplish? Details and exceptions accumulate. Soon the

---

*Computers can be programmed to operate *as if* they were functioning under conditions of uncertainty. In particular, a branch of logic, called "fuzzy logic," can be used to create programs that try to predict the probability of various outcomes when one or more pertinent conditions are not well known. However, at the level of the code itself, the logic is not fuzzy. Each programming statement must resolve into a set of executable machine instructions, each of which is logically determinant. If something unexpected happens at the level of the machine instruction, the chip has a bug or the computer is "broken."

beautiful crystal must be recut. This lovely edge and that one are gone. The whole graceful structure loses coherence. What began in a state of grace soon reveals itself to be a jumble. The human mind, as it turns out, is messy.

What has happened to the team so affably described by the vice president? The process moving so smoothly from left to right that it could be described without spilling a drop of red wine? It has become a struggle against disorder. A battle of wills. A testing of endurance. Requirements muddle up; changes are needed immediately. Meanwhile, no one has changed the system deadline.

The programmer, who needs clarity, who must talk all day to a machine that demands declarations, hunkers down into a low-grade annoyance. It is here that the stereotype of the programmer, sitting in a dim room, growling from behind Coke cans, has its origins. The disorder of the desk, the floor; the yellow Post-it notes everywhere; the whiteboards covered with scrawl: all this is the outward manifestation of the messiness of human thought. The messiness cannot go into the program; it piles up around the programmer.

Soon the programmer has no choice but to retreat into some private interior space, closer to the machine, where things can be accomplished. The machine begins to seem friendlier than the analysts, the users, the managers. The real-world reflection of the program—who cares anymore? Guide an X-ray machine or target a missile; print a budget or a dossier; run a city subway or a disk-drive read/write arm: it all begins to blur. The system has crossed the membrane—the great filter of logic, instruction by instruction—where it has been cleansed of its linkages to actual human life.

The goal now is not whatever all the analysts first set out to do; the goal becomes the creation of the system itself. Any ethics or morals or second thoughts, any questions or muddles or exceptions, all dissolve into a junky Nike-mind: Just do it. If I just sit here and code, you think, I can make something run. When the humans come back to talk changes, I can just run the program. Show them: Here. Look at this. See? This is not just talk. This runs. Whatever you might say, whatever the consequences, all you have are words and what I have is this, this thing I've built, this operational system. Talk all you want, but this thing here: it *works.*

Weeks later, I visited the vice president in her office. Behind her desk was a view of the salt fields edging San Francisco Bay. A watery atmosphere hovered over the bay, and the eastern hills were just visible through mist. I watched seabirds out fishing, planes lowering over the water on their way to the airport. High up in this tower, past the protocols of guards and security badges, was a sense of wideness and largeness, calm and distance.

The vice president was in charge of reengineering the company's global transaction processing. The vast network of banks, automated tellers, clearinghouses, computers, phone lines—all of which go into sending a single credit-card transaction around the globe—was her domain. On Christmas Eve 1995, her department processed seventy two million transactions. Three billion dollars whirred electronically across states, nations, oceans, and air. The very electronic backbone of capitalism: a universe of transactions, imagined money circulating on a planetary scale.

"If it all breaks down," she said, "the banks can't balance their accounts." She was surprisingly matter-of-fact about this catastrophe. "They might do business for a day, but they won't know what they're doing."

A wave of nausea washed over me: I imagined what it would feel like to leave a bug lying around and wind up being responsible for shutting down banks around the world.

"Can I meet the programmers who work on this system?"

She was uncertain for a moment. Then: "Well, yes. Maybe. Why not?"

"How many of them are there?"

"Three."

"Only three?" Another wave of nausea: the odds of being the one responsible for shutting down world banking were just increased to one in three.

The vice president laughed. "We're lucky to have them. The system is written in assembler."

"It's in *assembler?*" I felt a true, physical sickness. "*Assembler?*" Low-level code. One step above machine language. Hard to write, harder to change. Over time, the

comments begin to outnumber the programming statements, but it does no good. No one can read it anyway.
"How old is the system?"

"Fifteen years."

"Fifteen years! Oh, my God. . . ."

I trailed off and reconsidered the vice president, in her
plain but excellent suit, whose billions in electronic funds
were riding around the planet atop fifteen-year-old assembler code. Suddenly, I forgave her for saying that "programming is the smallest part of the process." I understood her
not wanting to dwell on the slip-space between the seventy
two million transactions and the tangled human-built logic
they must traverse. No, it's best just not to think too much
about the people who wrote the code. Just let it all "go off
to programming." Let three lucky programmers take care of
it. There: Gone. Done. Deployed.

When the vice president saw my sympathies, she
relaxed. Now she wanted to talk to me about all the
"groovy new technologies" being tried out by a special
programming group. Multitiered client-server, object-
oriented systems, consumer networks—all the cool stuff
that was on the opposite side of the universe from her
fifteen-year-old assembler code.

"We need all that new technology to handle the complexity," she said. "The number of transactions is growing
geometrically. The number of variables—the banks, their
needs—keeps accelerating. We want the programmers to
go off and be creative with all this new stuff," she said.

She was happy for a moment, imagining her domain

growing yet wider, yet busier, yet groovier. We both sat back and let the sexy glow of new technology overtake us. Then her mood took an abrupt shift. "But the programmers, the programmers. . . ."

She stopped, a dark look on her face.

"The problem is the programmers. Especially the ones working with the new stuff. Nobody can figure out how to manage them."

We sat quietly. The slip-space opened before us. The world and its transactions sat on one side. The programmers, the weird strange unherdable cats, roamed freely on the other. The vice president had peered into the abyss. Then she stepped back.

"Don't tell anyone I said that," she said.

Twenty years before my meeting with the vice president, I was a communist. I joined an underground party.* I took a nom de guerre. If I had been clever enough to write a bug fatal to world banking, I would have been promoted to party leadership, hailed as a heroine of the revolution. Nothing would have pleased me more than

---

*I quit the party after one year—I was expelled when I tried to leave. I then reviewed what I knew about computer programming and got my first job in the industry. My employer was amazed at my ability to work hundred-hour weeks without complaint, and I was promoted rapidly. He did not know that my endurance came from my year in the party. Being a cadre in an underground political party, as it turned out, was excellent training for the life of a computer programmer.

slipping in a well-placed bit of mislogic and—crash!—down comes Transnational Capitalism one Christmas Eve.

Now the thought terrifies me. The wave of nausea I felt in the vice president's office, the real fear of being responsible for her system, followed me around for days. And still, try as I might, I can't envision a world where all the credit cards stop working. The life of normal people—buying groceries, paying bills—would unravel into confusion overnight. What has happened to me, and what has happened to the world? My old leftist beliefs now seem as anomalous and faintly ridiculous as a masked Subcommandante Marcos, Zapatista rebel, son of a furniture-store owner, emerging from the Mexican jungles to post his demands on the Internet.

We are all hooked on the global network now, I tell myself, hooked to it and hooked on it. The new drug: the instant, the now, the worldwide. A line from an old Rolling Stones' song and an ad for an on-line newspaper keep running through my head:

> War, children,
> it's just a shot away, it's just a shot away.*

> The entire world
> is just a click away.†

---

*"Gimme Shelter," by the Rolling Stones.
†Advertisement for "The Gate," an on-line service of the *San Francisco Chronicle* and *Examiner.*

The global network is only the newest form of revolution, I think. Maybe it's only revolution we're addicted to. Maybe the form never matters—socialism, rock and roll, drugs, market capitalism, electronic commerce—who cares, as long as it's the edgy thing that's happening in one's own time. Maybe every generation produces a certain number of people who want change—change in its most drastic form. And socialism, with its quaint decades of guerrilla war, its old-fashioned virtues of steadfastness, its generation-long construction of a "new man"—is all too hopelessly pokey for us now. Everything goes faster these days. Electronic product cycles are six months long; commerce thinks in quarters. Is patience still a virtue? Why wait? Why not make ten million in five years at a software company, then create your own personal, private world on a hill atop Seattle? Then everything you want, the entire world, will be just a click away.

And maybe, when I think of it, it's not such a great distance from communist cadre to software engineer. I may have joined the party to further social justice, but a deeper attraction could have been to a process, a system, a program. I'm inclined to think I always believed in the machine. For what was Marx's "dialectic" of history in all its inevitability but a mechanism surely rolling toward the future? What were his "stages" of capitalism but the algorithm of a program that no one could ever quite get to run?

And who was Karl Marx but the original technophile? Wasn't he the great materialist—the man who believed that our thoughts are determined by our machinery? Work in a factory on machines that divide the work into pieces, and—*voilà!*—you are ready to see the social nature of labor, ready to be converted from wage slave to proletarian soldier. Consciousness is superstructure, we leftists used to say, and the machinery of economic life is the "base." The machines decide where we are in history, and what we can be.

During my days in the party, we used to say that Marxism-Leninism was a "science." And the party was its "machine." And when the world did not conform to our ideas of it—when we had to face the chaotic forces that made people believe something or want something or do something—we behaved just like programmers. We moved closer to the machine. Confronting the messiness of human life, we tried to simplify it. Encountering the dark corners of the mind, where all sorts of things lived in a jumble, we tightened the rules, controlled our behavior, watched what we said. We were supposed to want to be "cogs in a wheel."★

When the Soviet Union began to crumble, and the newspapers wrote about the men who controlled the

---

★Today's techno-libertarians have a similar idea about the mechanistic basis of human existence, but for very different reasons. They see human thought and consciousness merely as the result of many small, local processes in the body and brain, rather than as evidence of some observing self. While we communists wanted to make good fighting machines of ourselves ostensibly to further social equality, techno-libertarians prefer to see human life as a collection of small, local mechanisms because such mechanisms "prove" that controlling superstructures, like governments, are not necessary.

empire, I couldn't help noticing how many of them had been trained as engineers. Our country is ruled by lawyers, I thought, theirs by engineers. *Engineers.* Of course. If socialism must be "constructed" (as we said in the party), if history is a force as irrefutable as gravity, if a "new man" must be built over generations, if the machine of state must be smashed and replaced with a better one, who better to do the job than an engineer?

"I'm a software engineer," I reassured myself when I met the vice president, "an *engineer.*"

A week after seeing the vice president, I had lunch with the old friend who had recruited me into the party. We were talking about grown-up things—houses, relationships—when suddenly I couldn't stand it anymore. I reached across the table and asked her, "Did we ever *really* believe in the dictatorship of the proletariat?"

She looked at me like I was crazy.

I drove home through a tunnel and over a bridge, thinking about San Francisco earthquakes. I went home and thought about the gas line in the old Victorian flat where I used to live. We can't live without cash machines the way we can't live without natural gas, I thought. There is no way back. This is the fragility of what passes for regular life in the electronic era. We may surround that gas line with fancy moldings, all decorated with curlicues, yet it remains what it is: a slim pipe full of explosives.

What worried me, though, was that the failure of the global electronic system will not need anything so dramatic as an earthquake, as diabolical as a revolutionary. In fact, the failure will be built into the system in the normal course of things. A bug. Every system has a bug. The more complex the system, the more bugs. Transactions circling the earth, passing through the computer systems of tens or hundreds of corporate entities, thousands of network switches, millions of lines of code, trillions of integrated-circuit logic gates. Somewhere there is a fault. Sometime the fault will be activated. Now or next year, sooner or later, by design, by hack, or by onslaught of complexity. It doesn't matter. One day someone will install ten new lines of assembler code, and it will all come down.*

---

*On August 7, 1996, America Online became completely inoperational for nineteen hours, and its many subscribers had to face what life would be like without e-mail and access to the Internet. This one-day system failure was widely viewed as a harbinger of life in the electronic information age, the sort of occurrence that would become commonplace, given our reliance on computer-mediated communications. AOL's managers, however, described it as "a coincidental series of sequential events that will most likely never occur again." The problem was eventually traced to a software upgrade on a network router ("a bug in the operating system of the routers that was exercised by this particular routing"), the functional equivalent of installing ten new lines of assembler code. AOL's managers were right in a way. That particular problem did not happen again. The next failure came from too many subscribers trying to connect to the service, a monumental system jam described by the *Wall Street Journal* as "the busy signal heard around the world."

Brian can bring it all down. At least he'd like you to think so. He hangs out with a group of cryptographers★ dedicated to knowing how to bring it all down. Cypherpunks: that's what they call themselves. And if they have not yet brought the vice president's network to its knees, it may only be because Brian has advised an odd sort of patience. He has counseled his fellow rebel cryptographers to practice their skills quietly, watch while global networks get huge, and let system managers get complacent.

"You actually said that to a reporter!" I told him, "You said everyone should wait until there was really something big worth stealing!"

"Yeah," he answered with a grin, "I did say that, didn't I?"

★Computer cryptology is the study and practice of encoding information for the purposes of data privacy. This encoding is called encryption. Current encryption schemes involve the use of keys to scramble and unscramble the information. The longer the key — the more bits it has — the more difficult it is for an unauthorized person to decrypt the information. Encryption with longer keys is called "strong"; shorter keys result in "weaker" encryption. As of this writing, keys with 256 bits are considered uncrackable at the current state of the computing art. At the time of the conference discussed later in this section, the United States government, in an attempt to limit the dissemination of "uncrackable" information (and to make sure the FBI would be able to perform wiretaps), had made illegal the export of encryption software with keys longer than 40 bits. Currently the legal export limit is 56-bit keys and an encryption method called DES, but export of this relatively "weak" encryption is subject to obtaining a license from the Department of Commerce. In general, the U.S. government, through export controls, has hoped to control even the domestic use of encryption products, since such controls draw expertise and development energies toward weaker products.

Brian looks like a skateboarder. Or maybe he's what the devil would look like if the devil decided to move around among us disguised as a skateboarder. Brian has long dark hair, pale eyes covered by thick glasses, and a pointy little beard. He wears baggy jeans, a motorcycle jacket, and a black cowboy hat. At thirty-one, he has devoted what there is of his adult life to the absolute electronic privacy of money. His obsession about the privacy of wealth is like my generation's obsession about the privacy of identity, or sexuality, or belief, or the self.

In our industry, Brian is perfect. In appearing to be a genius on a skateboard, he couldn't be playing his part better. He looks exactly the way today's computing genius is supposed to look: boyish, brilliant, and scary. These traits alone almost recommend him for success, for Brian is in management in his second start-up company. Rebel cryptographers are just the sort of people venture capitalists want to give money to these days.

There's no good reason I should know any of this about Brian. If I had been going about my life in a sensible way, I should have done no more than notice him as once of those whiz-kid crypto types with their libertarian, multiple-partner lifestyles. In the normal course of things, when Brian approached me, I would have followed my first impulses and fled. Besides, in some cultures, he's young enough to be my son. But it was not a normal course of time for me, and I was not in a mood to be sensible. When I'm lonely for soul company, as I was then, I have a tendency to believe I'm open to anything. And sometimes this sense that I have nothing to lose makes me take risks I should not take, do things I should not do.

And I was in one of those risky moods. I'd spent two years in a series of loose-ended relationships. Before that, I parted ways with the woman I'd been with for eight years, and my father died, the two events coming within weeks of each other. All this is only to explain how, yes, I was lonely for soul company and, yes, I felt open to any-thing. And despite the known dangers of cavorting with libertarian cryptographers, I went off to a conference with the idea that anything might happen to me and why should I care.

Of course, such things have always happened at con-ventions. Even at conventions like this one: a meeting of programmers, hackers, EU policy wonks, German data privacy commissioners, representatives of the FTC, law enforcement geeks, software industry media stars—all there to debate issues of computers and civil liberties. But no one says that conventioneering techno-freaks are much different from conventioneering dentists. Both have their appropriate forms of funny hats, secret handshakes, and debauchery. Our form of debauchery was talk.

The real conference, the place to *talk,* was the hotel bar. There, on a very uncomfortable sofa, a mildly famous computing lawyer held forth night after night. And there, sitting knee-to-knee with him at the bar, I had late-night drinks with the Commissioner of Data Policy for Berlin. And over there, on the far side of the wide circular bar one late afternoon, is where I had my first real notice of Brian.

Brian was leaning on the bar, drizzling his long hair through his fingers as dreamily as any teenage girl. He was there doing what we all were doing: haunting the place to find some interesting *talk*. Maybe this was the one thing Brian and I had in common—this hunger for conversation, this hunt for an intelligent being with whom we might share our brain for twenty seconds.

At the time, I wasn't much interested in meeting Brian. Next to him was a man I really did want to meet, a writer of science fiction who had just spoken in the conference hall. After all the dull talk about data policies, he had delivered a jeremiad: about dirty words and dirty thoughts and the freedom for sons of bitches like himself to exist on the Internet. This writer was a grown-up man, a rebel of the kind I recognized: someone for whom saying "Fuck you!" into a microphone was the very essence of freedom. Besides, he was a man of words, not a technoid, and someone who clearly had his passions. But Brian, no. Brian could not be mistaken for a man with passions.

I recognized Brian as one of the cypherpunk crowd that had been sitting in a clump near the back of the conference hall. Whenever someone from the government or law enforcement spoke, they put up a wall of backtalk, a sort of peanut gallery of the cryptologically hip. Someone from law enforcement would inveigh against exporting encryption products with keys longer than 40 bits, and a guffaw would rise up from the cypher gallery. "We can break that," a voice would say, "No problem!"

"We need to be able to catch the bad guys," said the guy from the FBI.

Guffaws. Backtalk. Much flipping of long hair and pony tails.

"We cannot give powerful encryption keys to our enemies," said the commissioner from the Federal Trade Commission. "Exports must be limited to 40 bits."

"40 bits. *No problem!*"

Could they really crack any message encrypted with keys up to 40 bits, or would they just like everyone to think they could?★ Something in the whole cypherpunk presentation invited skepticism. The name they'd given themselves: punks. Their self-promotion. Their manifestos posted on the Web. The whole hip-boy-rebel thing. The idea that they could outsmart anyone: global superpowers, international law enforcement, giant transnational corporations—they hated any and all authority and no one was safe from their brilliant cypherpunkdom. And they were having way too much fun making everyone deeply nervous. Something about all this was just too familiar. Despite the techno-future glow of it all, something seemed old and recycled. It took me a while but it soon came to me: Yippies. They were latter-day Yippies. Jerry Rubin

---

★Evidently they, or people just like them, can indeed crack encryption with keys of 40 bits. At a data security conference held in January 1997, the conference sponsor, RSA Data Security, a maker of encryption products, offered prizes of up to $10,000 for breaking code encrypted with keys of various lengths. A Berkeley graduate student using 259 computers broke 40-bit encryption; it took him about three and a half hours.

and company with higher mathematics skills. *Steal this book! Crack this network!* Boys being bad: what else is new.

So it was that I had no particular interest in meeting Brian. When he drizzled his hair at me, I made my eyes slide off his immediately. When I kept running into him and he twice invited me to dinner, I declined, both times claiming to have already eaten. "It seems we are perpetually one meal out of phase, Brian," I said, which seemed to delight the mathematician in him. So I went elsewhere, several other elsewheres in fact, to indulge my openness to anything.

Why then did I return Brian's calls when I got back home? Maybe, despite those several elsewheres, I still had not played enough Russian roulette with my emotional life. Maybe I underestimated my own perversity. Most likely loneliness was a factor—and let's not forget flattery, because after all I am a woman of a certain age and Brian, to me, is a boy.

But these days, I tell myself a more intriguing story: that my interest in Brian had something to do with my being an old communist who builds software for hire. That it was somehow related to my attack of nausea over the vulnerabilities of international banking. That Brian—representative of everything my profession admires—was something I couldn't keep ignoring forever. And that this boy, with his pointy beard and octopus hair, was sent into my life as some sort of strange messenger, and his mission was to test me on what I believe in now.

[2]

BRIAN AND I AGREED TO MEET FOR SUSHI. It poured that night, an odd sort of rain for San Francisco, a steaming tropical downpour. It was all I could do to keep my raincoat around me, and through the gray wall of water that was the air, I barely saw the figure standing outside the restaurant. Motorcycle boots, wet leather jacket, straggled drenched long hair, cowboy hat with water running off the brim in torrents. Brian.

"Why are you standing outside in the rain!" is how I greeted him.

The restaurant was tiny, maybe eight tables. The air inside was close. Our eyeglasses steamed over in the humidity. I peeled off my wet clothes — raincoat, hat, scarf, jacket — and nearly ran out of chairs to drape them on.

I pushed up my shirtsleeves, looked over at Brian, and then, even before we'd seen a menu, I had time to regret that I'd ever agreed to this meeting. For Brian was giving me a gesture so bizarre, so inappropriate, that to this day I can hardly believe what I saw. His head was thrown back, his eyes were half closed. He sniffed at the air—once, twice, three times. Then he actually snorted. Though I'm sure I'd never seen anything like it in the whole of my life, I only needed to be a primate to understand its meaning: Brian wanted to fuck me.

I suppose it was outright amazement that kept me sitting there. How often, in a public restaurant, do you find yourself the object of someone's personal private masturbation fantasy? Because that is exactly what it felt like: as if Brian were all alone and I were some figment of his sexual imagination. But, as I said, I was in a risky place in my life. And if you pretend to be open to anything, these are just the sort of unsavory things that can happen to you.

For whatever reason, I resisted the impulse to pull on my wet clothes and dash back out into the rain. For whatever reason, I decided that it would be perfectly all right to spend the evening with someone who may have been brought up by wolves. I even convinced myself it might be interesting.

I was not immediately disappointed. Brian launched into talk about his work with the same wild unselfconsciousness that led him to a public display of sexual fantasy. And his vision of the Internet had the same quality of bizarre hyperreality—all the hallucinatory detail of a dream. It was like a dream of flying, only instead of soaring, we circled lower and lower, down toward the wires and machinery at the base of the Internet. For as "technical" as I might appear to my clients, as close to the machine as I was from their point of view, that's as far away as I was from Brian. He exploded the Net for me. I saw the many levels of hardware, each with its own software, its own little portion of intelligence. I was accustomed to thinking of a program as something that ran on a computer and of the network as only a means to carry messages around from computer to computer, program to program. But before we had even ordered our sushi, Brian had given me a vision of the Net as a complicated sea of intelligent devices, where the distinction between hardware and software began to blur and few people knew how to navigate.

Brian knew how to navigate. And because he knew, he would control the routes. He was quite straightforward about this: he wanted influence, and he wanted influence because he knew more than most people and because he was right. He would be the one to decide how a packet got routed. He would know where someone had clicked from and clicked to. He would decide who could have information about the way from one cyber place to some cyber elsewhere, and who could not.

"You're under non-D, right?" he said, looking up suddenly out of his reverie to notice that he had said things about his company that perhaps I shouldn't know.

"Right," I said, though I was much more ignorant than he imagined, and I could not have described his secret technologies if I'd wanted to.

One thing was for certain: neither government nor corporations were going to know very much in Brian's universe. The last time I had heard such off-handed rebellion, such naked disdain for big business and the government, was also from a long-haired man, another wildman who firmly believed in his own rightness. But that was 1969, and the man, twenty-three years old, was a member of SDS. Then, as if to turn my mind inside out, Brian abruptly turned to talk of business plans and initial public offerings, venture capitalists and marketing.

"Rebellion and money," I said, trying to sound nonchalant. But, inside, I was wobbling between past and present, between one long-haired man and another—and all the short-haired women in between; between socialism and software engineering; between the time of my own rebellion and the time of my money.

"An odd mix," I said, "rebellion and money."

"Oh, yes," said Brian, munching a pickle off his chopstick, "I'm an anarchocapitalist."

Anarchocapitalist. He said this with complete matter-of-factness. It was as if the statement required no further explanation, as if everyone was now an anarcho-capitalist, the way everyone was once against the war in Vietnam or into macrobiotics. Maybe these days everyone was indeed an anarchocapitalist, and it was only then— when I surfaced briefly from middle age to talk with Brian—that I'd noticed it.

At some point, Brian ordered our dinner—he seemed to know a great deal about sushi, and I sat passively and let him take care of it. What looked to me like an enormous quantity of raw fish now sat between us. Brian urged me to try a piece that he assured me would be particularly succulent. He picked one up for himself, popped it into his mouth, and was soon gone into a transport of pleasure.

"Oh, man," he said. He gripped the table. He shut his eyes. He lifted his head in a gesture of prayer. He swallowed. He smiled. "Have you tried this tuna? Oh, man! OH, MAN!"

Another feral moment. Another completely unself-conscious display. Again, I felt as if I'd caught him being alone. "I feel like I'm intruding on your pleasure," I said. "Should I leave?"

He grinned at me.

"You're very strange," I said.

"I used to think that was a compliment," he said. And his pleasure vanished.

It was at that moment that I thought there might be a bit more to Brian. Yes, he was weird. Yes, he barely belonged to this world. But a part of him knew all too well that he was odd, and he suffered from it.

We left the tiny sushi place. The rain had stopped and the streets had a steam-washed feel. I lived a few blocks away and intended to walk home. I gestured at the bus stop across the street. "There's your line," I said to Brian.

"Oh, no," Brian said, "I don't feel like I'm done talking yet."

Not done talking yet: this was indeed what we had in common. I am used to wearing people out; here was someone who had not yet had enough of me.

There was a wine bar near the bus stop, but Brian doesn't drink wine. There was a tapas place, but I knew it would be mobbed. I rejected all the quiet places for tea right nearby. I felt strangely vacant, as if my saner self could only watch as something inevitable happened.

I took him home.

"I mean," said Brian, facing me from the other end of the sofa, "have you ever really thought about what money is?"

This was why he came home with me, I realized. Oh, yes, sex, but before that would come the really important intercourse of tech talk. I was a programmer, I seemed to understand him, I had not run out of the restaurant despite his strangeness: all this recommended me to Brian. We sat with our legs extended across the sofa, not quite touching, and we were going to talk about electronic cash. I looked back through his thick glasses into terribly determined eyes, to a mouth set over that pointy beard. Had I ever really thought about what money is? No, but over the next terrifyingly intense hours—hours when the cross-bay trains would stop running and Brian, who had no car, would settle himself in—I was going to find out that Brian had indeed thought a great deal about what money is.

Brian's goal, indeed his mission in life, was to create an entirely anonymous global banking system. I'm not sure exactly why he wanted to do this, whether it was to get rich or to control the world or simply to prove that he could do it. In any case, he faced a rather serious obstacle:

he would have to deal with the entirely pesky problem of the United States legal system.

Brian's strategy, he said, was to "arbitrage existing law to set up a banking system without being a bank." That was his favorite word: "arbitrage." To Brian, "arbitrage" meant more than the traditional practice of buying and selling on a large scale to skim benefits from small differences between markets. He meant finding and manipulating the small skipped-over spaces in national and international law. Discovering the tiny interstices of the complex banking network that no one else thought much about. Locating a niche the laws had forgotten or that, in the new universe of electronic transactions, the law did not yet know about. Here he would set himself up, not illegally but extralegally, as a bank in essence not in law, in the place he knew where money "really" was, at the very heart of money.

In this place, anything might happen. The laundering of money, because there was "excess capacity in the Caribbean," according to Brian. The amassing of great riches by any means, all untouchable by governments, because here, in the Bank of Brian, we are between the rules of law.

Every time Brian said the word "arbitrage"—his mantra, repeated over and over—an image of Ivan Boesky, infamous arbitrageur, rose up in front of me. It was as if Boesky had regrown his hair and found his way to my sofa one rainy night. Boesky was everything I was brought up to hate. I come from a family of hard-striving New York small businessmen. No one was averse to taking his cut on a deal, but those commissions and brokerage fees and bonuses came after some actual good or service had been exchanged. My family came from the world where "stock" meant inventory, not paper. Nothing could have been more anathema to them, or to me, than the idea of someone like Boesky sitting in an air-conditioned room, watching a ticker, and picking off millions on the tiny differences between, say, the price of gold in London and New York. "Ach! Rats like Boesky are what make them come for us Jews," my father once said. "Scavenging!" is what he called it.

"Smuggling" was Brian's word for it: arbitrage as the ageless tradition of defying legal boundaries to carry desirable goods from a market where they're selling cheap to one where they're dear. The only difference was that Brian wanted to smuggle money itself, and he had no compunctions about it. On the contrary, he reveled in the very idea, turned it over and over in his mind, found in it an entire life philosophy. And there he sat on my sofa, drinking my tea, explaining, completely without apology, how he was going to "arbitrage" the United States legal code so that he could build himself a banking system that afforded complete privacy for wealth. A system that, incidentally, made the world safe for crooks, thieves, money launderers, and any average citizen who should just not feel like paying his taxes—a side effect of freedom, he said, the price of liberty, can't be helped.

"The system will be completely and mutually anonymous," said Brain. "No one will know what's in your account. And you won't know anything about the bank's finances. You won't know about their money and they won't know your balance."

Suddenly, something didn't seem right to me. "They won't know my balance?"

"Anonymous. Completely. On both sides."

Right then, I realized that I had not exactly brought home Ivan Boesky.

"So how will I get a statement?" I asked him.

Silence. Adjustment of eyeglasses. Drizzle of hair. "That's the responsibility part of the equation," he said. "You're responsible for keeping your own idea of your money."

"Are you kidding? Do you realize how few people can balance their bank accounts, even with a statement. How will accounts get reconciled?"

Longer silence. More drizzling of hair. Apparently, I was the first human being to listen to Brian long enough to ask a reasonable question.

"Well," he said finally, "obviously we'll need to do some more work on the infrastructure."

"Come over here," I said. "I'm cold."

Near my desk was a gas fire. I settled us in front of the fire then went to put on some music. "Early or late?" I asked. "What do you feel like, Palestrina or Beethoven?"

Another long silence. Another huge blank. "Classical music is not yet in my data banks," said Brian.

Now I wondered if he wasn't indeed brought up by wolves. Brian was the first technoid I'd ever met who didn't know music. Especially Bach and early music

47

—rule-based, pre-passionate music—standards in the defor-
mations of character that go into the making of a programmer. Maybe Brian really was a feral child.

I chose Spem in Alium, a sixteenth-century, forty-
voice motet by Thomas Tallis. Then I lay down on the
floor in front of the fire. Beside me, Brian stretched himself
along my side like a cat—he never touched me with his
hands. The music swelled up, massively polyphonic, forty
voices, each in its own part. Below a high, aching soprano
was a sound like everyone in the world talking at once.

After some minutes, I felt a light touch on my
shoulder.

"Turn it off."

"What?"

"Turn it off. Please."

I hit Stop; I heard him sigh. "Thanks. I began to hallucinate."

"Hallucinate?"

"It was just too much. I can't explain. I began to hallucinate."

I lay back down beside him. Mathematician who does
not know classical music. Cryptographer who can crack
information scrambled into nonsense by 40-bit keys—*No
problem!*—and he can't bear the sound of forty separate
human voices. I knew I should see this as a lack. I knew I
should see this young man as a case of hopelessly arrested
development. I should tell him to go sleep on the sofa
while I put on my crisp Brooks Brothers pajamas and got
some sleep. But again: there: I saw something more in him.

I saw that Brian was aware of this lack in himself, and that he suffered from it. Then, instead of dismissing him, finding him deficient, someone who could never give me the soul companionship I wanted, I betrayed myself utterly: I found him poignant. A wash of tenderness took me over. Right at that moment, with tremendous irritation at my own stupidity, I knew I would get involved with him.

His lovemaking was tantric, algorithmic. I once thought that love could not be programmed, but now I wondered. This sex was formulaic, had steps and positions and durations, all tried and perfected, like a martial arts kata or a well-debugged program. My own role in it was like a user-exit subroutine, an odd branch where anything might happen but from which we must return, tracing back to the mainline procedure. I felt again as if I'd come in on a private process, something that Brian had worked out all on his own and which, in some weird expression of trust, he had decided to show me. I should have felt dissatisfied. I should have called it off. For a time, I even looked fondly at the neat monogram on my pajama pocket where it lay on the dresser top. But again I betrayed myself: I gave in to curiosity and tenderness. He has been with himself too long, I thought.

Morning pillow talk with Brian was about transaction processing. It was not about parents or past lovers; I did not learn the numbers of his brothers and sisters, who his friends were, if he loved anyone. It was as if the hours of actual touch, the damp pillows and wrinkled sheets, did not intrude on our conversation.

Or, for Brian they changed everything. They freed him to race deeper into the obsessions he thought we shared. We lay in bed and discussed the Internet backbone. Wrapped in stained sheets, we pondered the expansion capacity of the global transaction processing network. Amidst the latex detritus of postmodern sex, we talked about the World Wide Web.

And of course we returned to arbitrage.

It seemed that art could now be arbitraged. Indeed, any content, any information, anything posted on the Web was now ripe for the skim. Said Brian, "See, the content no longer has any value. Who would buy a book when you could pick it off the Net for free?" Small moment of embarrassment as Brian remembered that I was someone whose work sometimes appeared in now worthless books. Then he moved on. "But the new value is in the transaction itself. The click. Every time someone clicks, someone makes money."

And it would not be the "content makers"—the artists, writers, multimedia makers—who would be making the money. Of course, the ones making the money would be the owners of the transaction itself. The new breed of entrepreneur: Net landlord. Content is worthless, art is just an excuse to get someone to click; meanwhile, artists watch their work circumnavigate the globe while "value arbitrageurs," the Brians of the world, pick off a fractional cent at every click, making a fortune.

"Is all this a good idea?" I asked.

"Sure. In principle. In a moral-less universe."

I imagined Brian's universe, anonymous stolen bits transmitted from node to node. At each node, a little program, a little bit of "moral-less" intelligence. Value arbitrageurs feeding freely, circling the Net like sharks in the Caribbean.

"Do you have morals?" I asked.

"Huh?"

"I said, Do you have morals?"

"Yeah," said Brian. But he waved his hands at me. It was clear I was interrupting a brilliant train of thought. He seemed disappointed in me. He thought I was smart, that I understood him, that I was technical and analytical. I think he even respected me for seeing the little flaw in his anonymous banking scheme; it made me interesting, challenging, a worthy companion. But now, in bringing up morals, I'd gone and ruined it: I'd brought up something dull.

"Oh, yeah," he said, still waving me off. "I have morals. But I don't want to get into that right now."

[3]

"TALK TO ME ABOUT OPERATING SYSTEMS," I SAID TO the property manager.

"I wish I could, sweetheart."

"Talk to me about software," I tried again.

"You know I can't, sweetheart."

I looked over at my sister. She is six years older than I am, once a huge gulf. But since the death of our father two years before, we'd become partners in the terrors of financial liability, which has a way of making people surprisingly appreciative of one another. "What do we know about this stuff?"

We were in a freezing basement restaurant in lower Manhattan. The stuff in question was a stack of papers that described, in great and incomprehensible detail, one hundred twenty-six arcane violations of the New York City building code. When my father died, he left the family two small commercial buildings in the Wall Street area. If it were up to my sister and me, we would sell these buildings, in all their state of violation, despite the small income they'd given us over the years. But our mother lives, in part, off the proceeds. And she also lives with the memory of my father telling her never, ever to sell the real estate. To him, these buildings, New York, Wall Street, represented everything of stable value in the material universe.

"They won't sign the lease if we don't clear the violations, dear," said the property manager.

I liked these buildings better when my father tended them, before I knew the buildings in all the realness of their real estate. I preferred them when they existed for me as paper, checks made out in my mother's neat Palmer Method script, sent monthly with little enclosed notes: "It was great to talk to you on the phone yesterday,—Daddy, dear." "Looking forward to seeing you for Pesach,—Mommie."

Earlier that day there'd been a steady, cold drizzle as my sister and I waited for the arrival of the property manager. It was afternoon and already dark. The streets were nearly deserted. From across the street, the black faces of empty storefronts stared back at us.

"At least we don't have empty stores," my sister said.

Thank God for that, I thought, aware it was the exact thing my father would say.

It was also what the property manager would say: he continuously scared us with the prospect of empty storefronts. Our buildings are around the corner from the New York Stock Exchange. When my father bought them, in 1961, they were in the very center of the capitalist world. Our "good" property is by the subway, where every morning legions of men in perfect blue suits once poured up the stairs and into the brokerages, onto the trading floors and up into the high-rises. They hired managers and underlings, secretaries and clerks, all of whom emerged at lunch hour to eat, buy handbags and shoes, dresses and suits, watches and knives. Then came the stock market crash of 1987. Then New York had its real-estate crash of the '80s, then its recession. Now we had the empty storefronts.

"Here you girls are," said the property manager, who came at us out of the gloom with a huge, too-bright golf umbrella.

"Here we girls are," I echoed. My sister and I have not been girls for a long time.

The property manager is only slightly older than we are, but he is a man of my father's world and time. He has the relentless, cheerful smoothness of the salesman, which makes me distrust him implicitly. But he is all that stands between us and the buildings. Our father told us almost nothing about his business dealings. All we know is we have inherited the properties; and we inherited the property manager along with them.

"The tenants are expecting us," said the manager.

My sister and I hate these ritual meetings. It's bad enough to be confronted with our ignorance of all things pertaining to real estate. But in meeting the tenants we must acknowledge to ourselves what we really are and really had been all those years of paper checks and little notes: we are landlords. Me: communist turned software engineer slash landlord. I'm no better than Brian, I thought. From this distance, Brian's schemes for owning the world seemed naive and almost sweet. His unregulated electronic universe seemed still promising, as if all its potential evils, unlike mine, still lay ahead and might yet be avoided.

We started on the upper floors. The office tenants are mostly Russian immigrants, refugees from the command economy who, all beknownst to themselves, have come all this way only to wind up the tenants of an ex-communist, something they could have done at home. There is a woman lawyer whose office is thick with cigarette smoke. Some odd company that gives questionable "training" seminars. Another Russian immigrant setting up a franchise for some strange health-food beverage in a foil pouch. (He pressed a sample on us; we demurred, then relented to be courteous.) My father was a sentimental man. He started up his accounting practice during the Great Depression. No doubt he saw himself in these boot-strappers. To me, though, their enterprises look fruitless and improbable — dying echoes of my father's old-fashioned burgher capitalism — all doomed.

On the ground floor are the stores: a tiny jeweler, a magazine stand, a shoe store, a dress store, a bag shop. Some have been tenants for twenty-five years. Almost all were behind on their rent. "What'll we do, kick them out?" said the manager. "At least we don't have empty storefronts." My sister and I exchanged looks. We decided to save the stores, in all their threatened emptiness, until after lunch.

It's here that we went down to the tiny cold restaurant. It's now that I had to consider the one hundred and twenty-six violations or risk empty stores. Old pipes. Asbestos insulation. Erratic sprinklers. Cracked sidewalks. Elevators that came too slowly and left too quickly. Stairways that had taken people up and down for decades and were suddenly declared to be too narrow.

"And who knows what else?" said the manager, "They go back to 1978." He made it sound like an eternity. We had to hire someone just to research the violations — a former building inspector who would get $100 per violation just to tell us what we had to fix. I imagined the labyrinthine corridors of the New York City buildings department, acres of ancient file cabinets guarded by surly civil servants. Our ex-inspector putting down his briefcase to keep his place in endless lines, slipping fifties here and there to "research" violations that may well turn out to have been written by the man himself.

"Now remember," said the manager, "that's $12,600 just for the research."

"How much will it cost to actually fix it all?" I asked.

"I wish I knew, kiddo."

"I feel like I'm stuck in a Borges story," I said to the manager's complete incomprehension. "Talk to me about software," I tried yet again.

"I wish I could, sweetheart."

The drizzly day, the dark storefronts, my confusion over being a landlord, the terror of losing the property, the hundred and twenty-six violations, the ex-inspector, the smiling property manager I can't quite bring myself to trust—it all just crashed in on me for a minute. I felt rage at my father for leaving us so ignorantly unprepared. I hated him for "protecting" us all those years. In the next instant, I yearned for the American-dream story I was brought up with: His mother, still 14 years old, escapes illegally out of Russia, supports herself in the sewing sweatshops. In the kitchen, she hangs up a portrait of Eugene V. Debs, and the old socialist looks down hopefully while my father goes to college during the Depression, starts his accounting practice, moves out of Bedford-Stuyvesant to Flushing, Queens, where he leverages ten thousand dollars, risking a million in debt, to buy himself a piece of Wall Street.

"Morty is expecting us," said the manager. Morty. The bag shop. The oldest tenant. The worst visit of all.

The store reeked of failure. It had an abandoned feeling, as though Morty, in his seventies, and his son, nearing fifty, hadn't left the place in twenty years. The stock was fashionable enough but it always had a dusty, disused look. Three blocks away, a huge discount chain couldn't keep enough handbags and wallets in stock, while Morty and his son sat in their empty store. Why don't they just give it up, I wondered? I could hardly think about the awful lack of choice that kept them sitting here year after year, asking for rent reductions, as their livelihood slipped away.

"It's the modems," said Morty.

What? Did he actually say this, or did I dream it. Was someone really going to talk to me about operating systems?

"Did you say *modems,* Morty?"

"Yeah. It's the modems. Used to be nice vice presidents took the train down from the East Side or in from Scarsdale. Now and then they bought a bag, a wallet, a briefcase. Now we get a different class of customer." He folded his hands over his belly and leaned back against the shelves behind the counter. "This class of customer—they want cheap, or they walk around and don't buy anything. Meanwhile the managers sit home in Connecticut. They don't pay city taxes and they don't buy bags. They telecommute, they call it."

He stopped, rubbed his arm. "It's the modems, I tell you."

I peered over at Morty, whom I'd clearly never seen before. This round old man in his empty store, for whom I'd never felt anything but pity, had just told me off in ways he could not imagine. He put it all together: Brian's networks, the bank vice president's universe of transactions, the software I write, the systems I install, the sexy bouts of software writing—all that was suddenly and clearly related to the world's financial center now all emptied of people. *It's the modems:* computing as a kind of neutron bomb, making all the people disappear, leaving the buildings.

In my world, it was so easy to forget the empty downtowns. The whole profession encouraged us: stay here, alone, home by this nifty color monitor. Just click.

Everything you want—it's just a click away. Everything in my world made me want to forget how—as landlord, as programmer, as landlord/programmer helping to unpeople buildings like my very own—I was implicated in the fate of Morty and the bag shop.

"You know," I said, picking up a wallet, "I think I need a new one."

"Morty'll give you a nice discount," said the manager, smiling.

Morty was not smiling and did not offer me a discount. I put down the wallet. "Maybe next time," I said.

"Now I'll show you the lofts," said the manager.

The lofts. They are in the other building, around the corner, above a tiny dress shop. They are wrecks. No one has used them for sixty years. The manager had some scheme where we "sell" a ninety-nine-year lease to a developer who improves the lofts then rents them as condos. "This area's so bad now, it's become ripe for residential," said the manager. "This way, you make less money but you turn the building into something like a bond. The developer deals with the tenants, and you get a fixed payment every month."

We climbed the dark back stairs. I stepped over loose floorboards. I looked at cracked windows, crumbling brick walls, falling-down tin ceilings, plugged chimneys. I inhaled dust from the days of my father's boyhood.

Was it possible: could this pile of decomposing matter really be turned into money?

"Sell them," I said.

"Sell them," said my sister.

"Do it," I said, imagining that I could go back to the years when my father was still alive and New York was still the middle of the capitalist universe. I convinced myself it was possible to go back to a time when sons of socialists could leverage their way into big deals and real estates, so that, years later, ex-communist programmer consultant daughters, living far away in California, could clip their coupons by electronic transfer. I imagined I really could turn this collection of mortar and bricks into a kind of bond, not a thing but an asset, that I might undo its very realness, convert it into something that will come to me in one of Brian's dustless, encrypted, anonymous, secure transactions. It would be money freed of ancient violations and struggling tenants, distilled into a pure stream of bits traversing the continent at network speed, just a click away—hardly money at all, but some new measure of value: logical, dematerialized, clean.

"We're setting up an offshore porn server," said Brian.

We were having dinner together a few weeks after my return from New York. Brian stopped eating and waited to see my reaction.

"In Mexico," he added.

The Mexican waiter serving us tapas put a plate on the table and seemed to freeze there. Finally the waiter let go of the plate and walked off.

"It's our way of raising venture capital," Brian went on. Again he waited for my reaction, grinning, in a kind of dare.

I waited for my own reaction, and waited some more. Eventually it came tumbling at me from all directions. But, outwardly, as far as Brian was concerned, I had not moved. Finally, to do something, I shrugged. "None of my business," I said. Shrug.

My reaction tested, Brian disappeared into the arcana of his cross-border traffic. In his usual dreamlike detail, he talked about anonymous remailers and other network deception tricks I promised to keep secret but which I could not explain if I wanted to. The whole complicated business of international pornography had devolved, in Brian's thinking, to the level of a mathematical problem, some famously difficult proof, a challenge of the mind. He seemed neither attracted to nor repulsed by the content of the stuff he would be sending around. To him, it was just bits, stuff on the wire—my building turned into a bond or a picture of a woman tied up and raped—none of his business either.

Meanwhile, tapas getting cold in from of me, Brian spinning dreams of techno-deception, I replayed my reaction to myself. *Shrug.* I cast off twenty years of feminist debate. *Shrug.* The battles of my mid-twenties, the groups of women dividing and subdividing over this issue. The slogans, the shouting matches: Sexual freedom! Take back the night! Anti-sex! Pornography hurts women! A decade when I was in collectives large and small, in parties and formations and factions, all of them intending to change the world. *Shrug*. I let it all go. How could he understand anyway? Why go into all that now? *Shrug*. All the old politics fell away so easily, like scales off a dead fish. And what did it matter? I had no particular liking for what Brian was doing, but I couldn't imagine a world I'd want to live in where it should be illegal. The argument could only be moral, some private decision a person must come to alone, and, right then, just come from a round of landlording, I was fresh out of moral superiority.

"Who'll do the groundwork for you?" I asked, to change the subject. "Setting up an office, leasing, getting phone lines. I mean, it's not exactly Switzerland. Do you know Mexico at all?"

No, Brian had never been to Mexico. He didn't know that Mexico was one of the last places on earth where a wall mural of Che Guevara is not pop art. But his business partner knew the country and "had the corruption problem all figured out," according to Brian. Their plan was to set up servers in two cities just across the border. When the police in one city asked for bribes, they'd say that the police in the other would take less. "We'll play the police in one city off the police in the other," said Brian. "We'll say, 'If you don't cut this deal, we'll just pull the plug and do business elsewhere.'"

Brian picked up an olive, studied it, and ate it the way he ate sushi. "Man! Don't you just love olives! OH, MAN!" Then he sat back in his chair with a look of immense satisfaction. "That way we deal with corruption by using arbitrage."

Arbitrage. That word again. What a useful concept. It seems there's a way to make money from everything.

"We're arbitraging corruption," he said. The thought amused him thoroughly. Pop: another olive. Then he laughed.

[4]

I'M UPSET, SO I'M TAKING APART MY COMPUTERS. If I were a poet, I'd get drunk and yell at the people I love. As it is, I'm gutting my machines.

My computers are not broken, but at times like these I like the look of delicate circuit boards open to the naked air. Several hours ago, in a fit of restlessness, I decided to install a pre-release version of a new operating system. Then there seemed to be problems with some of the internal devices. So I took them out, one after the other. Now they lie all around me—cards, wires, memory modules, screws—all in a jumble. To test components, I do what I'm absolutely not supposed to do: run the machines with the covers off. I'm supposed to discharge static electricity before touching anything. But I scuff around on the carpets, grab things with two hands, hold metal to metal. I recognize the nastiness of this mood, reckless and rebellious, like I could get away with breaking the laws of physics.

There's a perverse comfort in broken machinery.

Even as things get worse—for a time I can't even get to the power-on self-test—I look forward to the mean mood I'll be in while I tinker. I have a tendency to curse broadly when hardware and software won't work. I take their malfunctioning as a personal slight. "Stupid fucking engineer," I mutter to the guy who wrote the code. "How could you be so blind?" I think of the stupidity as a male sort of perfectionism, a refusal to plan for a user's small inattentions or mistakes. If women designed machines, begins my thought, imagining maternal allowances for the electronic equivalents of spilled glasses of milk. But immediately I let the thought go. There's no denying that I suffer fools as badly as anyone, female though I am. Like any of the boy engineers, I *enjoy* cursing at the machine. It makes me feel superior: smarter than the hardware, smarter than the software, smarter than everyone who built it.

The last screw goes in and the system boots up. The drives spin up to speed and fill the room with a sound like sighs. *There,* I think, my edginess leaving me. *It works. . . .*

I was not ready to think about Brian. I especially didn't want to think about the fact that, after the dinner where I learned about his porn server, I went home with him, and we had hours of sex, night and morning. The truly difficult thing to accept was how good it was. I don't mean only the physical pleasure of bodies and positions, but a certain presence to one another, a certain close attention, which does not happen as often as people imagine it does. So it was all the more confusing to find it there, with this too-young man, who had no real emotional ties to me, or me to him, and whose values I found disturbing.

This time, the sense of mechanism and distance was gone, and in its place Brian showed surprising awareness: to the small cues that say *yes there* and *more here* and *no more*. And there was a genuine sweetness in him, a still-not-cynical hope for the communion of sex and a sense of its extraordinariness. We talked. We made love. We talked more and made love again. We wanted to please each other. And we did. And later, as we slept, when he let go of me for a while, he apologized.

By the next evening, back home in my own life—not certain if or when I would ever see Brian again—I was sorry I had seen that sweetness. It was easier to think of him as a selfish brainy kid. I preferred the idea of him as some fascinating cyborg. If he was sweet and could be present, then he acquired realness, and his sudden realness released something wholly unexpected in me. It was a scary starved ferocity that came pouring out: for men, for the great dark otherness of sex with them, for the whole night side of me I'd shut down so I could stay for eight years with a very kind woman. And somehow this was mixed up with my attraction to Brian's very unsweet side, to his "moral-less universe" so defiantly selfish, an attraction that might have been a type of liberty, or a form of self-destruction, or both. I found myself in the

car, radio loud enough to cause pain. "You are the perfect drug, the perfect drug, the perfect drug," went the
song, but the "you" was no one in particular; or it was
me, seen from a long way off and through a suspect
memory.

I had taken this whole thing far too lightly. I had
entered this belief-test on a lark. While I was busy
unearthing what Brian thought of the world, I'd run
smack into something I believe most unshakably: there is
no such thing as a casual relationship.

Another thing I didn't want to think about was my
building, which did not turn into a bond. As much as I
wanted it to become a financial instrument, the building
remained solid, material, hopelessly real. Even worse, to
cover the brokerage fees and the costs of clearing the violations, we had to take out a loan. In the end, we didn't
receive checks; we sent them.

Meanwhile, the property manager seemed to have
lost interest in our lofts. "I'm into a deal on a smart building," he told me on the phone. "You know, all wired up
for little companies like yours." I tried explaining to him
that I'm not much of a company, but he was in full blush
of first technophilia: "T1s and ISDNs in every room, and
what-do-they-call-it? Etherset—"

"Ethernet."

"That's right, Ethernet. In every room. Plugs—"

"Jacks."

"What about your father, dear?"

"No. I didn't say 'Jack.' I said 'jacks.' They're not called 'plugs' they're called 'jacks.'"

"Whatever. We got it. This plug and that jack. Too bad your building isn't. . . ."

"It isn't a smart building."

"No. It isn't. It just isn't—"

"—not suitable for high-tech start-ups."

"No, it's not. But it is a—"

"—landmark—"

"—a headache! Why did your father—"

"Why did my father buy a landmark? Oh, he was proud to own a landmark. He loved New York. He was thrilled to own a piece of it, and a landmark! A building with a plaque! He sent me a picture book—"

"He sent me the same one, with the picture—"

"Yeah. Of the building—"

"—which you now cannot touch the outside of because it's a—"

"—landmark."

"A landmark! *Headaches!*"

Months later, the property manager's "smart building" wasn't nearly leased. It seems there aren't enough "little companies" like mine to fill up all the emptiness of Wall Street. Money may move at the speed of electrons, but properties and cities, streets and buildings, change on the scale of human generations. My family will have to sit tight; the lofts will remain dust.

Even Wall Street wants to leave Wall Street now.

Some months after I got back from New York, I read an article in the *Wall Street Journal:* the New York Stock Exchange needs more space for its computer equipment and is talking about moving out of the city. More empty storefronts loom on Wall Street, on the actual Wall Street, the place that once anchored a city. What will they call it, I wondered, after they move: www.wallstreet.com?

But why shouldn't the Exchange move away? Why shouldn't the market makers live like the vice presidents, telecommuting from nice homes in Connecticut? The NASDAQ is just a big computer system, so why not the NYSE? The building at Wall and Broad, just around the corner from us, might perhaps be turned into a tourist attraction. Maybe some actual traders could stand on the floor in traders' shirts and shout into microphones for voice-recognition transmission into the system. Why not? Cities seem to have turned into franchised amusement parks. Megastores on Times Square, the very same Virgin and Gap and Disney stores on Union Square in San Francisco, on the Plaça de Catalunya in Barcelona, along the Champs-Élysées. The same Levis and Mickey Mouses and *hamburguesas.* So why not an NYSE megastore?

Brian is right about money: there's no need for us to hold it anymore. Bits on wires, units of something transferred between electronic accounts—that is the true nature of money. There's no longer a need for marble palaces and pillared properties. Morty and his son and their bag shop should just set themselves up on the Internet.

Last week I went to an old downtown branch of my bank. Although this branch is the closest one to where I live, it's not *my* branch. As one of the tellers explained, the concept of an account having a "home branch" is obsolete. The portion of the account number that used to be coded as the home branch is now just an account category. "You can be anywhere and bank anywhere!" the teller exclaimed.

Like my father, I can't resist the lure of city centers. He had his office steps from Fifth Avenue and 42nd Street, and bought his first building around the corner from Wall Street; and, like him, I like the sense of being in the middle of human activity, the idea that everything passes by and anything might happen to you there. I take the trouble to bypass the drive-up ATMs elsewhere, I walk through actual streets with real humans walking on them, all to get to my downtown palace of money. Its entrance is a pillared rotunda. Granite steps shadow the curve of the rotunda. Inside heavy brass doors is a plantation of marble pillars. The ceiling looks like gold. To open their stations, the tellers push back little gates of glass edged in bronze. A small bronze lamp circles each station in a private pool of light. We wait in an aisle of velvet ropes. Then, in a dim echoey hush, we exchange slips of paper, our money and its representations, with all the solemnity of a Eucharist.

After I finish my business, I linger for a while. There is a bench made of carved marble. The arms are curved and decorated, the back ornate. On the seat and back are cushions of fine brown leather. I sit down. I rub my hand along the smooth, cool arm. I think about a time when children sat on this bench while mothers waited for hallowed transactions in the velvet line. I remember going to the bank with my own mother: the sound of her high heels on marble, the suggestive dark of the little room where she retrieved jewelry from her safe-deposit box. I recall the scent of her perfume, White Shoulders, as it rose, heated, in the closeness of the little room, in the excitements of jewels and marble and money.

The world has no use for all this anymore, I think. Women don't wear perfume just to go to the bank, and money doesn't live in vaults with twirling handles like ships' helms. Money lives in Brian's universe of e-cash, as everyone at my bank knows, as they rush past me toward a line of ATMs at the far end of the vast room, which look bizarrely metallic and sleek in this marble cathedral of cash.

Which bank is "real": the one of marble or the one with silvery sleek technology? Neither, as Brian understood. Both are constructions designed to reassure us. *You can trust us. Give us your money.* Once we were impressed by buildings; now we are impressed by virtual on-line spaces, that's all.

Perhaps in the new on-line banks, we will each be able to create our individual idea of money, our personal private virtual bank-space where we can mix whatever we wish into the excitement of money. It can be a world like my first night with Brian: all externalized masturbation fantasy. Yours can look like a white-cube art gallery, yours a secure spare vision of double-doored Eurobanks, mine a robber baron's idea of opulence. In my bank fantasy, I walk through streets crowded with pedestrians: beautifully dressed Parisian women with their thin, thin legs, their lovely soft boots fastened at the ankle; gentlemen of sixty from Barcelona, in long, pencil-slim cashmere coats, cigarettes in gloved hands; handsome Italian men of twenty-five, camel-hair coats draped on shoulders and flying behind them like capes. At the entrance to the bank, up the granite steps below the rotunda, will be two beggars, two perfectly typecast homeless people (click here to give them money), just a small dose of discomfort, so that I sigh with relief as I push open the heavy bronze door and step into the vast dim hush of my money.

But what about the high heels, I wonder. How will I hear the full reverberation of those heels on marble? And the strangers—the light voyeurism of watching other people transact with their money. And the sense that I am in the middle of the world and anything might happen to me here. How will all this happen to me, once I am safe at home, and everything has been flattened to two dimensions, a screen, a keyboard, and a mouse? And—oh! — what about the White Shoulders?

No one but me sits on the beautiful marble bench. The bank guard eyes me, circles me, slides his hand along his belt. I want to say something like, "Nice day, isn't it, sir?" but surely this is something I've seen in an old movie. I stand up, zip up my jacket, pat my wallet, and leave.*

At least the AIDS project is going well. After my years of writing software used only by other software, the ingenuity of the human user fascinates me. There are bugs, but the users, with their great, mysterious, accommodating intelligence, avoid them. The entry of certain pre-fifteenth-century dates will crash the system. "Well, we just don't put in those dates!" say the users, quite reasonably.

Within a month, some hundred AIDS patients get registered. Everyone is happy—too happy. It worries me that no one has refused to sign the consent-to-share forms. Everyone confronted with a sheath of legal papers, all requiring signatures, has duly executed them: I hereby agree to share my records with all other participating agencies. I herein acknowledge that I have been given the option to deny such permission but have declined such. I agree to take part in an evaluation. Yes, a salesman may call. Said one patient, "I have AIDS. I'm on SSI. Big Brother already has my number. So what else do I have to sign?"

I worry that I have given the system too cute a name.

---

*Two months after I had my banking fantasy, I went to a conference at which a financial services company, Liberty Financial, demonstrated an Internet-based program for its customers. The program was "customizable," said the company representative, to give customers what he called a "personalized, interactive experience." Banking as electronic fantasy game is undoubtedly coming, but the company's product needs work; my fantasy is better.

My client wanted to call it the Centralized Intake, Registration and Information & Referral System, the bureaucratic and non-euphonious C-I-R-I-R-S: "sear ears." But I insisted on something "modern." In a meeting, I told them that the state of the art is to name a system after a person. Thomas—I brought up the Congressional system named for Thomas Jefferson. Was there someone who really wanted this system, I asked them, some early advocate?

They were disappointed. For some time now, they had been referring to the system as CIRIRS. A gloomy silence fell over the conference room.

"There was Philippe," said someone finally.

"Philippe! Perfect! I speak French. I would be delighted to build something named Philippe."

"Too fancy," said someone at the next meeting.

"Too *French,*" said someone else, with a certain *tone.* We all heard it: something was going on that had nothing to do with fanciness or France, some political infighting thing that nobody wanted to touch. There was dead quiet, into which Philippe, the system, disappeared.

"There's Reginald Green," someone suggested at last. And it was all but settled on the spot. Reginald was an activist, he had AIDS, and what's more, he was black. Reginald. Reggie. Also short for registration. Magical combination of the linguistically fit and the politically correct.

So it was that I came to build a system named Reggie. Who could be afraid of a system named Reggie? In case of some lingering hesitation, I gave it pretty guacamole-colored screens, and, on the first two screens, the ones where

users log on and select a task, a scanned-in picture of a smiling African-American man with AIDS: Reggie.

I've done my job too well, I think. No one is suffi-
ciently wary of this system.*

I also gave it access to the Internet. And e-mail. And
a Usenet news reader. And zippy ISDN phone lines. All
the trendy new World Wide Web software, necessary
hallmarks of the state of the art—all that became the
"information and referral" components of the original
sear-ears idea. I tell myself I'm saving the client money by
not programming a referral system. I tell myself I'm drag-
ging the nonprofit sector into the era of late-twentieth-
century computing. I argue that, if corporations have all
these goodies, why shouldn't social service agencies also
have digital phone lines and fast Pentiums, LaserJets and
edge routers, wide-area networks and great big host-end
controllers. And if every entity in the world is about to
have a Web home page, well, why shouldn't Reggie?

When I watch the users try the Internet, it slowly

---

*On May 9, 1995, auditors from the federal Inspector General's office
entered the offices of a Boston AIDS-services provider and compiled
a list of names, Social Security numbers, dates of birth and HIV status
of 98 patients. The provider protested that the taking of the information constituted "an egregious breach of confidentiality." The federal
government maintained, however, that the service provider received
federal funding and therefore the government had a right to audit
patient data. According to a report in the *New York Times* (April 3,
1996, A13), the auditors said "there was evidence of fraudulent use of
Social Security numbers and that they reported that [fact] to other
federal officials responsible for investigating such fraud." The federal
government's right to confiscate files was later upheld in court.

becomes clear to me that the Net represents the ultimate dumbing-down of the computer. The users seem to believe that they are connected to some vast treasure trove—all the knowledge of our times, an endless digitized compendium, some electronic library of Alexandria—if only they could figure out how to search it properly. They sit and click, and look disconcertedly at the junk that comes back at them. Surely it must be their fault, they reason; surely if they just followed the right links, expressed their query more accurately, used another search tool, then pages and pages of interesting information would soon be theirs. And so their clicks become more insistent for a while. Soon, however, they start tumbling: What link have they followed? Where are they? They click "Back" then "Back" again, and, like players in a Victorian maze retracing their steps, they emerge to find they are only at the place where they entered.

In front of a spreadsheet, however, their helplessness and confusion vanish. When users want to show me the sort of information they have been storing, they open elaborate, intricate spreadsheets full of lists and macros and mathematical formulas, links to databases, mail-merge programs, and word processors. They have, in effect, been programming. I am amazed at the ingenuity shown in putting together these many tools. I am astounded at the complexity managed so deftly by these "naive" end users.

What is it about the Internet, with its pretty graphics and simple clicks, that makes users feel so inundated; and about the spreadsheet—so complicated a tool—that makes them bold? The received wisdom about user-friendliness is challenged here. Human beings, I think, do not like to be condescended to.

The spreadsheet presumes nothing. It has no specific knowledge, no data, no steps it performs. What it offers instead is a complex vocabulary for expressing knowledge. It is, literally, a blank sheet of paper with a notion of columns and rows—and everything held on that sheet is presumed to come not from the program but from the human user. In the relationship between human and computer that underlies the spreadsheet, the human is the repository of knowledge, the smart agent, the active party. The user gives data its shape—places it in columns and rows, expresses the complex relationships among those columns and rows—and eventually turns data into more knowledge. It is the end user who creates information, who gives *form* to data, who *informs* the spreadsheet.

The relationship between person and machine is completely reversed on the Internet. The Net is the knowledge repository, and the user can only search it.*

---

*The same could be said of a library, except that libraries have something the Internet considers nearly anathema: librarians. The current reigning ideology of the Internet is strictly opposed to the idea of a librarian's overriding sensibility, opting instead for the notion that anything, in and of itself, is worthy content. So it is entirely up to the end user to distinguish junk from literature. Hence the rapid proliferation of search engines. It is interesting to note that, over time, the search engines themselves are beginning to incorporate biases and strategies that could be characterized as ordering sensibilities. However, these strategies are not in the public domain, in a sense making each search engine a private card catalog, a personal collection.

The information on the net is predigested—all laid out in "pages," all linked, albeit arbitrarily and chaotically. To shape this unwieldy, untended library into something meaningful requires the active participation of the user—but Internet browsers do not offer the rich and expressive vocabularies of spreadsheets. Users get buttons to press. They can go "Back." They can go "Home." They can create links. That's it: the vocabulary of a five-year-old confronts the vast, messy archive that is the World Wide Web.

The spreadsheet is the program that all but created the personal computer. The spreadsheet and the word processor—two tools empty of information, two little programs sitting patiently and passively for their human owners to put something interesting into them. Now, fifteen years later, the Internet browser is the program creating the second generation of the personal computer. The browser—a click-click baby tool for searching the Web, where everything of interest already resides. It is a journey through the looking glass in the age of information: one pill makes you larger, and one pill makes you small.

Am I doing the users a favor? What information have I really given them by providing access to the Internet? The project does have one Internet success almost immediately. A patient asks about a prescription for a new drug. The provider doesn't know it. Click on the link to the Centers for Disease Control, and there it is: actually useful information. But the success story soon becomes apocryphal. I hear my client tell it over and over at planning meetings and realize: that's it, there will be no other success stories. "Oh, I don't find it much use," says one user. "Well, I've used it for personal stuff," says another, the henna-haired, red-nailed director of the women's clinic. She blushes, but only a little. After all, we're grown-ups hard at work at ground zero of a of sexually transmitted, deadly, epidemic disease. Maybe Brian is right; maybe there's nothing to do but shrug. A little recreation couldn't hurt.

In the end, the Reggie home page all but gives up on the idea of being a resource link to information on the Net. Instead, we supply information about the AIDS service providers participating in the project. Never mind that the clients Reggie is supposed to serve are not likely to have a computer, let alone a connection to the Web. Forget about that nasty reality: having a Web page has become the way we must prove our existence. We have a "presence" on the Web: we are therefore real. Click here to learn all about Project Reggie. Here are our hours and services. Come use us, we say. In the end, we simply do what everyone else does on the Net: we advertise.

I begin to wonder if there isn't something in computer systems that is like a suburban development. Both take places—real, particular places—and turn them into anyplace.

I once lived three blocks from an undeveloped hillside. The land was scrubby, dry, left wild because the base of the hill was slowly being carved out by a working stone quarry. The steady beep-beep of backing trucks broke the quiet, dust rose continuously from the quarry, and the fifty-mile view from the top was toward the plebeian southern end of the city. Still, the hill had an austere beauty. Hawks would glide down the slopes, out hunting rodents in the thick growth of mesquite and poison oak. Deer trails crisscrossed the fire roads. Once I saw a mountain lion. Maybe the appeal of the place was simply its human emptiness, and even when I didn't hike up the fire trails, it comforted me just to know the hill was there.

Then one day I noticed that bulldozers were cutting off the hump of the hill. Soon it was clear that not even the quarry could hold off development forever: a housing tract was coming. The trails were closed, the groan of bulldozers joined the sound of beeping quarry trucks, and the houses began going up. When the development was nearly done, I went up to the top of the hill—or what was left of it—driving this time.

What struck me was how normal it looked. Ranch houses along regularly curving streets. Double garages. Blacktop driveways. Barely anything to describe—that's how much it matched the idea of "suburban housing development." Even the sense of being on a hill was gone, the view now being the sole province of the houses along the "cliffside," presumably more expensive. How had they done it, I wondered? How had they taken that wild, scrubby place, in all its particularity of hawk and deer and poison oak, and turned it into a paradigm place, a standard set, an anyplace?

Something similar happened with the AIDS project. Despite the idealism of the programmers, the good intentions of my client's staff, the hard work of the users, what we created in the end was not the "system of care" we set out to build. In the end, what we created was only a system.

The first sign was the users' problem with e-mail. Connecting the providers via electronic mail was supposed to "increase communication," "facilitate information exchange," and other worthy organizational goals. My client spoke glowingly of imagined charts and files attached to friendly e-mail messages, all circling from agency to agency, enwrapping the patient in an electronic blanket of service. But it didn't exactly turn out that way.

"I worry that e-mail is breaking down our system of care," said one user.

"Is it a training issue?" asked my client. "Do you need another e-mail course?"

"No," said the user, "the problem is we used to talk on the phone a lot. Now we don't."

"Oh."

"We relied on knowing each other. Now we don't."

"Oh."

Now they can sit in the office like programmers and send e-mail. Now they can stay where they are like stock analysts and connect by modems. Oh.

Next came budget and scheduling wrangles. Could the second phase of the system be done in December? At first, I tried what may be the oldest joke known to programming managers—"Sure you can have it in December! Of what year?"—but my client was in deadly earnest. "There is a political deadline," they said, "and we can't change it." It did no good to explain that writing software was not a political process. The deed was done. They had gone around mentioning various dates—dates chosen almost at random, imagined times, wishes—and the mentioned dates soon took on an air of reality. To all the world, to city departments and planning bureaus, to task forces and advisory boards, the dates had become expectations, commitments. Now there was no way back. The date existed and the software would be "late." Of course, this is the way all software projects become "late"—in relation to someone's fantasy that is somehow adopted as real—but I didn't expect it so soon at the AIDS project, place of "helping people," province of "good."

I asked, "What part of the system would you like me not to do?"

"You tell us," they said.

"This one. This piece here can't be done on time."

"But we must have that one! It's a political requirement!"

Round and round: the same as every software project, any software project. The same place.

All the "goodness" was slowly draining away. Then, two months into the planning of the second phase, the project took a distinctly "bad" turn. The director of the department began asking for links between client registration data and other city systems. She wanted to compare delivered services to commitments in providers' contracts. She wanted cross-checks on funding sources, billings, contract compliance. She wanted to run the client information against a database kept by a group ominously called "Surveillance."

"I thought the idea was to improve client care," I said.

In meeting after meeting, I argued with the director. I tried to warn her that the machine cannot keep rounded edges; that its dumb, declarative nature could not comprehend the small, chaotic accommodations to reality which kept human systems running. How would it help clients if Reggie told her that this particular underfunded agency should be even more underfunded? What good would it do to find out that this poor, ill person was not quite as poor and ill as he was supposed to be? How would it help if, in the awful and explicit way of computer systems, Reggie made clear what everyone knew—that there was a little fudging going on around the edges, so that providers could get a little extra and give a little more. In the absence of the machine, everyone could wink at these small rough edges. But Reggie—cute little Reggie with its guacamole-colored screens and the smiling face of an African-American man with AIDS—could make it all plain beyond deniability. "Don't do this," I said to the director. "Once you have this information, you'll have to do something about it."

But she was adamant. "The people paying for this system have a right to good data!" she declared.

In this way, the system became the justification for the

system. We collected data, therefore it had to be "good" data. And since we could link one database to another, since it was possible to cross-check data here with data there, well, we should link them. And what was designed to store patients' information as a service for *them,* had somehow become the property of the "people paying for this system"—an agency of the federal government.

I didn't really blame the director. She was a progressive woman who worked desperately hard to move the sluggish environment of the civil service. Reggie was her idea; it could not have existed without her. And there was nothing sinister about her motivation to account for all of the taxpayers' money. No, she was a fine and energetic professional. She had simply done something I'd seen too many times before: she had succumbed to the fever of the system. As a product manager once told me, "I've never seen anyone with two systems who didn't want us to hook them together."

I remembered the first time I saw a system infect its owner. It was early in my career, at my first software company. I had just installed a new system at the offices of a small business in Central California. It was a sleepy place, a quiet city surrounded on every side by irrigated fields, in the great water-poor agricultural valley of Central California. The offices were on a two-lane road, in a plain single-storied building with a parking lot.

The company's employees had been there for ten and twenty years, particularly the women, mostly clerical workers. They were the ones who would be most affected by the new system, yet they went about learning it with a homey cheerfulness that surprised me. I had the impression that these women of fifty or so were approaching the computer as it truly should be treated: as some new and nifty kitchen appliance with which one could make really swell things. All that was necessary, their good humor suggested, was to follow the recipes carefully.

The installation went smoothly. Later, after the women returned from training, I visited the office again. The business owner, an apparently good-natured Rotarian, was heartily pleased with his new computer. He insisted upon taking me out to dinner.

Normally, I would not much want to eat dinner with an independent insurance agent at the revolving restaurant atop a Holiday Inn. But there was no way to refuse. And the client, whom I'll call William Banner, turned out to have a hearty, Protestant-ethic sort of charm. "Good job!" he kept saying, "You did a good, good job. Now order the steak!"

Our table went slowly round and round, I ate my first steak Bernaise (too rich), we drank what I, gratefully, did not then recognize as a truly dreadful red wine, and William Banner had nothing but nice things to say to me. I thought I was going to get through the evening pleasantly. But just after we ordered dessert, Mr. Banner leaned over to me and asked, "Can you keep track of keystrokes?"

We had been discussing the local produce markets. "Keystrokes?" I asked.

"You know, on the computer. The keys. Can you keep a record of every key someone enters?"

I was so surprised by this question that I believe we went through a quarter-circle revolution before I answered. "Well, yes. You could. Yes, there are ways to do that."

"What would it cost us to do it?"

"To keep keystrokes? I don't know offhand. But why? Why would you want to do that?"

William Banner dug into his ice cream, which had just been put down before him. "Well, take Mary. I'd like to know everything that Mary does in a day."

Mary was the receptionist and general office manager. She was William Banner's oldest employee, twenty-six years. As I recalled, Mary knew every one of the company's clients by name. For the first several years of her employment, when Mr. Banner's kids were small, she used to pick them up from school, take them home, and pour them milk.

"But why do you want to keep on eye on Mary? She's doing very well with the system. I mean, is there a problem?"

"Oh, no. No problem," said William Banner, "but, you know. . . . Well, I'm just curious. All those years she's been out there running things, and now I can find out exactly what she does."

"So you want to know about Mary just because you can?" I asked.

William Banner swirled his ice cream around like a kid, then licked a big wad off his spoon. "Hmm. That's it, I suppose. The way I look at it, I've just spent all this money on a system, and now I get to use it the way I'd like to."

I watched William Banner finish his dessert and coffee, and a certain dizziness came over me, as if we were suddenly revolving too quickly. What if he found out that Mary made mistakes, as she surely did? What would he do if he didn't like the way she did the invoices before the checks, the account reconciliations before the journal entries? Would he intervene minutely in her working day? Would he risk upsetting twenty-six years of loyal service? Would he wind up *firing* her?

"I don't think keystroke monitoring is a good idea, Mr. Banner," I said.

"Eh?"

"Keystroke monitoring. It's a bad idea. The system is a tool to help people do their work, not a watchdog. If people feel they are being watched, they put their creative energies into hiding things."

"Oh, well, that's possible. But when I saw the system running, I thought to myself, 'I bet this thing can tell me what everyone is up to all day.'"

The system was installed, it ran, and it spoke to him: you can know every little thing you always wanted to know. You can keep an eye on the woman you trusted to pick up your kids from kindergarten. You can count every keystroke, and you want to count them simply because it's possible. You own the system, it's your data, you have power over it; and, once the system gives you this power, you suddenly can't help yourself from wanting more.

"Your system installation has gone extremely well,

Mr. Banner. I can't recommend too strongly against this idea of keystroke monitoring."

"Well, I could always hire a local kid to do it."

"Well, I suppose you could."

Many years and clients later, this greed for more data, and more again, had become a commonplace. It had become institutionalized as a good feature of computer systems: you can link them up, you can cross-check, you can find out all sorts of things you didn't set out to know. "I bet this thing can tell me what everyone is up to all day," said the insurance agent whose employee of twenty-six years knew all his customers by name. "The people who own this system have a right to good data!" said the woman who had set out to do a favor for sick people.

I'd like to think that computers are neutral, a tool like any other, a hammer that can build a house or smash a skull. But there is something in the system itself, in the formal logic of programs and data, that recreates the world in its own image. Like the rock-and-roll culture, it forms an irresistible horizontal country that obliterates the long, slow, old cultures of place and custom, law and social life. We think we are creating the system for our own purposes. We believe we are making it in our own image. We call the microprocessor the "brain"; we say the machine has "memory." But the computer is not really like us. It is a projection of a very slim part of ourselves: that portion devoted to logic, order, rule, and clarity. It is as if we took the game of chess and declared it the highest order of human existence.

We place this small projection of ourselves all around us, and we make ourselves reliant on it. To keep information, buy gas, save money, write a letter—we can't live without it any longer. The only problem is this: the more we surround ourselves with a narrowed notion of existence, the more narrow existence becomes. We conform to the range of motion the system allows. We must be more orderly, more logical. Answer the question, Yes or No, OK or Cancel.

Our accommodations begin simply, with small workarounds, just to avoid the bugs: "We just don't put in those dates!" said the very sensible users of the Reggie system. Then, slowly, we incorporate the whole notion of systems: we'll link registration data to surveillance, to contract compliance, thought the director. Finally, we arrive at tautology: the data prove the need for more data! We think we are creating the system, but the system is also creating us. We build the system, we live in its midst, and we are changed.

I had been on the AIDS project for a year and a half; it was time to move on. "I don't think I'm long for this job," I told the director.

"I understand," she said, relieved, I think, to see me go.

I am saved by a phone call. Two consultants I've worked with before have recommended me for a contract. Would I like to talk about designing a networking management tool, asks the caller.

It's a start-up company that has been taken over by

its venture capitalists—"VCs," as they're known. When many millions have been invested in a company, and there is still no prospect of taking it public—and the VCs believe they have a product worth saving—they send in the salvage squad. This time the salvage squad is a man and woman my former colleagues once worked for. The woman is an heir to the fortune of a large paper company—she turns trees into Chanel suits, is how my consultant friend put it. The man is her usual right-hand-man, a guy who rolls up his sleeves and learns how to log on to the system. Once he can log on and look around at the software, he fires the company's executives and managers, then fills in until he can hire new executives and managers. In the interregnum come the consultants—me and people like me.

The office has the disheveled, temporary-encampment look of any start-up recaptured by the VCs. Old files are stacked in cartons along the walls. A Ping-Pong table has been set up in the empty space where the partitioned cubes of fired employees have been taken down. The corner offices are empty. In the kitchen are stacks of Diet Pepsi, mounds of bagels, moguls of cream cheese—all the signs that the programmers who have not been fired rarely leave the place.

My interview takes barely half an hour. I'm hired, and immediately I am released from the indignity of end-user-dom. This time, on this contract, I will be working only with programmers and networking people. As to what flows over the networks—it's no longer any of my concern. Let them send information about sick people or nudie shots. *Shrug*. None of my business. I will be paid some egregiously large sum of money plus fully vested stock options to give advice on the way the program should look and operate. As I sign the nondisclosure agreement, I remember the lie I told my acquaintance who has her own venture-financed company, the lie I let her believe. Start-up company. Networks. Non-D. Watch out what you lie about: your lie may come true.

10:30 AM: programmer commute hour on the freeway. South toward Silicon Valley, the remnants of the fog are just lifting off the bay, and the sky breaks through, a washed-blue-jean blue. Four sparsely filled lanes, stock-option sports cars like mine pushing 80, delivery vans riding at the limit—a freeway the way God meant it to be. The car in front of me tailgates everyone out of the way, then zooms off. The carpool lane, defunct at this hour, has turned back into the fast lane, and its painted diamonds stretch out ahead for miles.

"Can you edit this field?"

"No."

"Then it should be a—"

"Oh, yeah. A different control—"

"A label."

"Yeah."

"And what about finding devices for connections?"

"Well, that's a binary operation—"

"You're right. These other operations here are all—"

"Unary."

"Right. Unary operations. So should we—"

"—represent them with the same interface?"

"Or is there something distinct about—"

"—about binary operations."

"Yeah, so we should define some other—"

"—some other interface paradigm."

Nine hours with the programmers go by and I have no sensation of time passing. When I glance at the window, I'm surprised to see that the light is oblique and the sky's blue has deepened. My first day on the new contract has come and gone, and it's as if I've always worked there, so quickly do the programmers and I find our common language. Now I drive north back to the city, and again I've missed the traffic. My little car hums along at an effortless 75. I play a Vivaldi chorus—loud—on the CD. Just as I round the edge of the bay, the last lines of fog are catching the edge of the sunset, writing a furious red calligraphy across the sky. The city glows in the last light, the sky darkens and—*Magnificat!*—the red strokes blaze above the skyline.

I can't believe I get paid to do this.

[5]

It had to happen to me sometime: sooner or later I would have to lose sight of the cutting edge. That moment every technical person fears — the fall into knowledge exhaustion, obsolescence, techno-fuddy-duddyism — there was no reason to think I could escape it forever. Still, I didn't expect it so soon. And not there: not at the AIDS project, where I fancied myself the very deliverer of high technology to the masses.

It happened in the way of all true-life humiliations: when you think you're better than the people around you. I had decided to leave the project; I agreed to help find another consultant, train another team. There I was, finding my own replacement. I called a woman I thought was capable, experienced — and my junior. I thought I was doing her a favor; I thought she should be grateful.

She arrived with an entourage of eight, a group she had described on the telephone as "Internet heavy-hitters from Palo Alto." They were all in their early thirties. The men had excellent briefcases, wore beautiful suits, and each breast pocket bulged ever so slightly with what was later revealed to be a tiny, exquisite cellular phone. One young man was so blonde, so pale-eyed, so perfectly white, he seemed to have stepped out of a propaganda film for National Socialism. Next to him was a woman with blond frosted hair, chunky real-gold bracelets, red nails, and a short skirt, whom I took for a marketing type; she turned out to be in charge of "physical network configuration." This group strutted in with all the fresh-faced drive of technocapitalism, took their seats beneath the AIDS prevention posters ("Warriors wear shields with men *and* women!" "I take this condom everywhere I bring my penis!"), and began their sales presentation.

They were pushing an intranet. This is a system using all the tools of the Internet—Web browser, net server—but on a private network. It is all the rage, it is cool, it is what everyone is talking about. It is the future and, as the woman leading the group made clear, what I have been doing is the past. "An old-style enterprise system" is what she called Reggie as I had built it, "a classic."

My client was immediately awed by their wealth, stunned silent by their self-assurance. The last interviewee had been a nervous man in an ill-fitting suit, shirt washed but not quite ironed, collar crumpled over shiny polyester tie. His entire programming career had been spent in the nonprofit sector, doing desktop programming. For him, the AIDS project would have been a large technical step up. He was eager and attentive and respectful. Now here came these new visitors, with their "physical network configuration" specialist, their security expert, their application designer, and their "technology paradigm." And they came with an attitude—the AIDS project would be lucky to have them.

It was not only their youth and self-assurance that bothered me, not simply their high-IQ arrogance (at one point, to our disbelieving hilarity, they proposed fingerprinting AIDS clients "to help with the ID problem"*). It wasn't just their unbelievable condescension ("For your edification, ma'am," said one slouch-suited young man by way of beginning an answer to one of my questions). No, all this was common enough. I'd seen it before, everywhere, and I'd see it again in the next software engineer I'd meet. What bothered me was just that: the ordinariness of it. From the hostile scowl of my own programmer to the hard-driving egos of these "Internet heavy-hitters": normal as pie. There they were on the cutting edge of our profession, and their arrogance was as natural as breathing. And in those slow moments while their vision of future Reggie was sketched across the whiteboards—intranet, Internet, cool, hip, and happening—I knew I had utterly and completely lost that arrogance in myself.

I missed it. Suddenly and inexplicably, I wanted my arrogance back. I wanted to go back to the time when I

---

*Given the political nature of the project, a certain degree of ambiguity in the identification of clients was considered an acceptable price and was designed into the system. However, the most technically capable consultants uniformly suggested ID cards and fingerprinting as "solutions" to this ambiguity of identity. It became a sad joke: if they suggest fingerprinting, we said, they probably can do the job.

thought that, if I tinkered a bit, I could make anything work. That I could learn anything, in no time, and be good at it. The arrogance is a job requirement. It is the confidence-builder that lets you keep walking toward the thin cutting edge. It's what lets you forget that your knowledge will be old in a year, you've never seen this new technology before, you have only a dim understanding of what you're doing, but — hey, this is fun — and who cares since you'll figure it all out somehow.

But the voice that came out of me was not having fun.

"These intranet tools aren't proven," I found myself saying. "They're all release 1.0 — if that. Most are in beta test. And how long have you been doing this? What — under a year? Exactly how many intranets have you implemented successfully?"

My objections were real. The whole idea wasn't a year old. The tools weren't proven. New versions of everything were being released almost as we spoke. And these heavy-hitters had maybe done one complete intranet job before this — maybe. Probably they were getting by with many late nights spent fiddling with code. But in the past none of this would have bothered me. I would have seen it as part of the usual engineering trade-offs, get something, give up something else. And the lure of the new would have been irresistible: the next cover to take off, the next black box to open.

But now, no. I didn't want to take off any covers. I didn't want to confront any more unknowns. I simply felt exhausted. I didn't want to learn the intranet, I wanted it to be a bad idea, and I wanted it all just to go away.

"And what about network traffic?" I asked. "Won't this generate a lot of network traffic? Aren't you optimizing for the wrong resource? I mean, memory and disk on the desktop are cheap, but the network bandwidth is still scarce and expensive."

More good objections, more justifications for exhaustion.

"And intranets are good when the content changes frequently — catalogs, news, that kind of stuff. This is a stable application. The dataset won't change but once a year."

Oh, Ellen, I was thinking, What a great fake you are. I was thinking this because, even as I was raising such excellent issues, I knew it was all beside the point. What I was really thinking was: I have never written an intranet program in my life, I have never hacked on one, I have never even seen one. What I was really feeling was panic.

I'd seen other old programmers act like this, get obstructionist and hostile in the face of their new-found obsolescence, and there I was, practically growing an old guy's gut on the spot. But the role had a certain momentum, and once I'd stepped on the path of the old programmer, there seemed to be no way back. "And what happens after you leave?" I asked. "There just aren't that many intranet experts out there. And they're expensive. Do you really think this technology is appropriate for this client?"

"Well," answered the woman I'd invited, the one I'd

thought of as my junior, the one I was doing a favor, "you know, there are the usual engineering trade-offs."

Engineering trade-offs. Right answer. Just what I would have said once.

"And, like it or not, this is what will be happening in the future," she said. "This is where all the new tools and languages are headed."

The future. Right again. The new: irresistible, like it or not.

But I didn't like it. I was parting ways with it. And right at that moment, I had a glimpse of the great, elusive cutting edge of technology. I was surprised to see that it looked like a giant cosmic Frisbee. It was yellow, rotating at a great rate, and was slicing off into the universe, away from me.

"What do you think?" asked my client after the presentation.

We sat, exhausted, beneath the AIDS posters. What did I think? What did it matter if I was staring down the road of my own obsolescence. I was leaving anyway. "Hire them," I said. "If you can afford them, hire them."

I learned to program a computer in 1971; my first programming job came in 1978. Since then, I have taught myself six higher-level programming languages, three assemblers, two data-retrieval languages, eight job-processing languages, seventeen scripting languages, ten types of macros, two object-definition languages, sixty-eight programming-library interfaces, five varieties of networks, and eight operating environments—fifteen, if you cross-multiply the di[fferent combinations of operating systems] and networks. [I don't think this makes me particularly] unusual. Given [the rate of change in computing, anyone] who's been aro[und for a while could probably make a list] like this.

This proc[ess of remembering too-soon-gone] is a [just] like trying to r[emember all your lovers, you have to root] around in the [past and wonder, Is that all? Have I missed] anybody? In s[ome ways, my professional life is made] uniquely suited [to the technologies] [it] [created—serial] monogamist—[long periods of intense engagement punc]tuated by time[s of great change and searching. As hard] as this may be [on the emotions, it is a good profile for] technology.

I've man[aged to stay in this perpetual state of learning] only by maintaining what I think of as a posture of igno-rant humility. This humility is as mandatory as arrogance. Knowing an IBM mainframe—knowing it as you would a person, with all its good qualities and deficiencies, knowledge gained in years of slow anxious probing—is no use at all when you sit down for the first time in front of a UNIX machine. It is sobering to be a senior pro-grammer and not know how to log on.

There is only one way to deal with this humiliation: bow your head, let go of the idea that you know anything, and ask politely of this new machine, "How do you wish to be operated?" If you accept your ignorance, if you

[handwritten margin note: being perpetual / not being able to log on / & perpetual learning]

really admit to yourself that everything you know is now useless, the new machine will be good to you and tell you: here is how to operate me.

Once it tells you, your single days are over. You are involved again. Now you can be arrogant again. Now you *must* be arrogant: you must believe you can come to know this new place as well as the old—no, better. You must now dedicate yourself to that deep slow probing, that patience and frustration, the anxious intimacy of a new technical relationship. You must give yourself over wholly to this: you must believe this is your last lover.

I have known programmers who managed to stay with one or two operating systems their entire careers—solid married folks, if you will. But, sorry to say, our world has very little use for them. Learn it, do it, learn another: that's the best way. UNIX programmers used to scoff at COBOL drones, stuck year by year in the wasteland of corporate mainframes. Then, just last year, UNIX became old-fashioned, Windows NT is now the new environment, and it's time to move on again. Don't get comfortable, don't get too attached, don't get married. Fidelity in technology is not even desirable. Loyalty to one system is career-death. Is it any wonder that programmers make such good social libertarians?

Every Monday morning, three trade weeklies come sliding through my mail slot. I've come to dread Mondays, not for the return to work but for these fat loads of newness piled on the floor waiting for me. I cannot possibly read all those pages. But then again, I absolutely must know what's in them. Somewhere in that pile is what I must know and what I must forget. Somewhere, if I can only see it, is the outline of the future.

Once a year, I renew my subscription to the Microsoft Professional Developer Network. And so an inundation of CD-ROMs continues. Quarterly, seasonally, monthly, whenever—with an odd and relentless periodicity—UPS shows up at my door with a new stack of disks. New versions of operating systems, database software, developer libraries, development tools, device driver kits—everything you need to know to keep pace with Microsoft. The disks are barely loaded before I turn around and UPS is back again: a new stack of disks, another load of newness.

Every month come the hardware and software catalogs: the *Black Box* networking book, five hundred pages of black-housed components turned around to show the back panel; *PCs Compleat,* with its luscious just-out laptops; the *Programmer's Supershop,* "your voice for Internet, client/server and networking technologies"; and my favorite, the *Programmer's Paradise,* on the cover a cartoon guy in wild bathing trunks sitting under a palm tree. He is all alone on a tiny desert island but he is happy: he is surrounded by boxes of the latest programming tools.

Then there is the *Microsoft Systems Journal,* a monthly that evangelizes the Microsoft way while handing out free code samples. *The Economist,* to remind myself how my libertarian colleagues see the world. *Upside, Wired, The Red Herring:* the *People* magazines of technology. The daily *Times* and *Wall Street Journal*. And then, as if all this periodical literature were not enough, as if I weren't already drowning in information—here comes the Web. Suddenly, monthly updates are unthinkable, weekly stories laughable, daily postings almost passé. "If you aren't updating three times a day, you're not realizing the potential of the medium," said one pundit, complaining about a online journal that was refreshing its content—*shocking!*—only once a day.

There was a time when all this newness was exhilarating. I would pour over the trade weeklies, tearing out pages, saving the clips in great messy piles. I ate my meals reading catalogs. I pestered nice young men taking orders on the other end of 800 phone lines; I learned their names and they mine. A manual for a new tool would call out to me like a fussy, rustling baby from inside its wrapping. I took it to bed, to the kitchen table; I read it at nights, on weekends. There was no satisfying this desire to know, and yet to know more. The fact that there seemed to be no end to the things one had to know was all the better. It was like riding in a powerful car in the days of cheap gas: more, faster, now.

What has happened to me that I just feel tired? The weeklies come, and I barely flip the pages before throwing them on the recycle pile. The new catalogs come and I just put them on the shelf. My machines are three years old—ancient by my own standards. I haven't loaded my last two Microsoft distributions; I tell myself it's because I'm having a problem with the CD-ROM drive. The invoice for the Professional Developer subscription just came from Microsoft: I'm thinking of doing the unthinkable and not renewing.

I'm watching the great, spinning, cutting edge slice away from me—and I'm just watching. I'm almost fascinated by my own self-destructiveness. I know the longer I do nothing, the harder it will be to get back. Technologic time is accelerated, like the lives of very large dogs: six months of inattention might as well be years. Yet I'm doing nothing anyway. For the first time in nineteen years, the new has no hold on me. This terrifies me. It also makes me feel buoyant and light.

It could just be my age. I'm middle-aged, a time for consolidation, deepening what you know, ignoring distractions. Time tells me to stop chasing after the latest new everything. Biological life does not want to keep speeding up like a chip design, cycling ever faster year by year.

And maybe there is something unseemly in an old programmer. Maybe the isolated compulsion of coding, its bottomless details, its narrow-well horizon—the sheer electric nervousness required for a relationship with the machine—is simply unnatural for someone over thirty-eight. Maybe an old programmer is like an old Mick Jagger. Past a certain age, it just won't do to keep sticking out your tongue and singing "Satisfaction."

Then again, the problem may just be too many updates to Microsoft Windows.

A few months ago, I went to a Microsoft Professional Developers Conference. It was just after the company woke up to the possibilities of the Internet. They had been pushing a minor Web scripting language called Blackbird, which they decided to kill off, also killing off countless little Blackbird companies that had been racing to start themselves up.

Microsoft had a new plan. What had started as the scripting language for a desktop tool called Access had by then evolved to the Visual Basic language, which became something called embeddable VBX controls, which became OCX controls operating under OLE and Networked OLE; which, at this very conference, had just evolved into ActiveX controls under Distributed OLE. Which, if you wanted them to interoperate with Java applets, you had to use under DCOM, Microsoft's proprietary version of CORBA.*

"It's almost getting to be too much," said a voice behind me on the escalator.

I turned around. A man. Gray streaks showing in his

*The acronyms refer to evolving models for what are called software "objects" as promoted by Microsoft and Sun Microsystems. Software objects are designed to let one program, such as a charting tool, be embedded in another, such as a spreadsheet. They also permit small application programs, called "applets," and even finer-grain collections of code, to be shared over a network, including the Internet. At the time of this writing, Sun and Microsoft were offering competing, incompatible object models.

pony tail. The beginnings of a paunch. Not a kid but not yet my age. The guy next to him was younger by ten years. Maybe it was just the older guy's age. Maybe time did indeed explain everything.

"How do you take it?" asked the younger one, the one without gray streaks or paunch or middle age. "How do you keep up?"

I strained to hear the answer, but the escalator was carrying us down to the conference floor, where Microsoft product managers were explaining how to "drill down" layer after layer into the heart of the operating environment, down and down into the new. The noise rose up at us, and the reply was swallowed into the general noise, into the general anxiety of unlearning Blackbird and relearning VBX, into the panic of letting go of OLE and embracing DCOM.

So I never did hear the older one explain how you get used to it after a while, how it becomes normal to discard your certainty and hunker down into the newest thing, how it is no fun but there is a certain perverse satisfaction in reorienting your brain at a right angle to its previous position. And there, lost, you go ahead anyway. And there, somehow, you make it run.

"We're pitiful," said Mark, the database programmer.

"Pitiful," said Sam, another database consultant I'd hired to work with us.

It was somewhere in the middle of my time on the

AIDS project. Mark, Sam, and I were trying to configure a database. We sat in the heat of the tiny machine room, nearly stupefied by fan noise and machine exhaust. Three hours had gone by. The database was still not configured.

What was taking us so long? We each had over ten years of experience. We were all early employees of the company that had built the database software we were configuring. By any measure, we were experts. Still, a certain parameter escaped us. A certain setting stumped us. A certain option sent us hunting through the manuals. Then the manuals couldn't help. We called other experts, other early employees of the company that built the database software, each with over ten years of experience. They didn't know the answer either.

For a moment: guilt. Three meters running by the hour: experts are expensive. We should know this, I thought. I imagined other, better experts who could do this job more quickly. But the guilt passed. I'd been doing this long enough to know that, pitiful as we were, we were it. The three of us struggling through the running of this database on a new operating system, flipping through incomplete documentation, using trial-and-error settings of options—this was what passed for expertise in our business.

Finally a setting seemed to work. We started a configuration process, and we sat watching the screen. We talked bored programmer-talk as text scrolled up on the monitor.

"I'd like to be doing Java programming," said Mark.

"Java?" I asked. "Who'll pay you to learn Java?" Java was then a barely known computer language. It was the newest fashion, the language of the Internet. We all knew we'd have to learn it, but no one knew exactly how or when. "We've already forgotten our SQL," I said, "and we're barely fluent in C++. Do we have to move on to Java already?"

Mark and I exchanged looks. We both came of age using a programming language called C, and neither of us felt comfortable in its successor language, C++. But Mark didn't like me to talk about this fact.

"I'm learning Java from Randy," said Mark. "He's an old Java-head."

"Old Java-head?" I asked. "How old a head can he be? Java itself is only a year old."

"Oh, Randy learned it way back in May."

We were having this talk in September. "Oh, way back in May!"

"Well, that's old these days."

"Yeah," I said, "Ancient."

"Shit!" said Sam. "Device allocation failure!"

"Try changing the partition size—"

"No, it's the device name. Change the device—"

"No, I think it's the logical name, not the physical drive."

"Yeah, it conflicts with—"

"Shit! You're right."

The experts went back to fiddling. Many settings later, the configuration was completed successfully, and the project had a database. Eight months later, Mark had indeed became an old Java-head. The last I heard, his time was being billed at $160 an hour. He was not short of work.

The corollary of constant change is ignorance. This is not often talked about: we computer experts barely know what we're doing. We're good at fussing and figuring out. We function well in a sea of unknowns. Our experience has only prepared us to deal with confusion. A programmer who denies this is probably lying, or else is densely unaware of himself.

The awareness of my own ignorance came to me eight years into my career. I was still working for the company that built the software we were configuring at the AIDS project. I was having trouble getting a particular monitor to work with our software. I called the manufacturer of the monitor. I called the supplier of the keyboard. I called the company that wrote the device driver software, that built the mouse, that wrote the operating system. I received many answers, all contradictory. Somewhere through my fourth round of phone calls came two thoughts in horrifying succession. The first thought was: I suppose I know the answer better than anyone else in the world. The second was: I don't know what the hell I'm doing.

Over the years, the horrifying knowledge of ignorant expertise became normal, a kind of background level of anxiety that only occasionally blossomed into outright fear. Still, the fear was a great motivator. The desire to avoid humiliation was a strong concentrator of the attention. I even came to rely on it. When I interviewed Danny, the desktop programmer, to work on the AIDS project, I knew he had less experience than he was letting on. I knew he was taking on this job out of sheer will. But I hired him anyway. I did it because I saw the fear in his eyes.

I told Mark, "The new guy is afraid."

"Oh, good," said Mark, "then he'll work out nicely. If you're not terrified in this profession, you really don't know what you're doing."

"Open App Studio and get to the project," said the lead engineer on my new contract. It was my second day. He had never seen a resume or my company brochure or talked to me about my experience. But it would never have dawned on him that anyone could be working as an engineering consultant without complete and utter knowledge of Microsoft Visual C++, Version 4.2, Professional Edition.

I looked at the screen. Everything on it—the tool, the language, the library they were using—had come into common use after I stopped programming full time. Since then, I had become what I was on this project: a designer, a manager, a maker of schedules and budgets. In the regular world, these responsibilities would be considered promotions. And I was certainly making more money than I used to. But this was not the regular world. The people I had to direct were programmers, and nontechnical managers don't get away with directing programmers for very long. When they meet you, there is really only one thing programmers want to know: are you technical or not?

I squinted at the code. It was the bizarre, ugly syntax of the C++ language. I came of technical age with its predecessor, C, which I could read and write like English, which I could debug just by having it read to me over the phone. But here it was as if I were a native speaker of Spanish trying to read Portuguese. Yes, the roots were the same, yes, these are the same words, but where had all these strange letters come from? How had this word turned into that? Clearly this language came from the other side of some political and cultural schism, a new and unknown country where I could just get by. "Thorny stuff," I said, speaking sentences from a traveler's phrasebook.

The programmer hovered over me in the small cubicle. He was as high-strung and twitchy as any programmer I'd known. He literally bounced, elbows flapping. He felt like an electric buzz behind me.

This was my test: Was I technical or not? Could I be the engineer of last resort? When he had a problem, was I going to be any use to him, or was I just another pain in the neck telling him what to do?

He waited. I scrolled through the code. Then I scrolled some more. Object-oriented software: small hunks of code, understandable only if you know a whole hierarchy of logic. Tiny window, fifty-line viewport, to see little blocks in an elaborate pyramid. Murk and confusion.

But just then some blessed instinct took over, a subliminal skill still there after all those years of reading code. Something surfaced, miraculously, out of the murk.

"Here it is," I said. "Here's what you're looking for."

"Where?"

"Here. This CGXView thing."

"Oh great! So we can put the grid in a view."

"Yeah. Not just in a window."

That was it: test over. I gave him his chair and he immediately set to programming, his knees opening and closing, opening and closing, as if he were some huge, manic clam. I was sweating. But I had passed. For one more day at least, I would still be thought of as "technical."

I remembered a birthday party many years ago. The woman who would become my partner of eight years ordered the cake for me. It arrived in a huge box that all but filled the table. This woman gathered the guests around and made a big fuss about everyone being there to see the box cover opened. Everyone waited. She lifted the cover. She beamed. There sat an enormous sheet cake with a greeting scripted in lemon butter cream. It said: "Happy Birthday, Senior Engineer Ullman."

I held a small, white, spiral-bound book. I waved it at Brian. "In here was the entire UNIX operating system," I said, "all of it, down to the bottom."

We were sitting on the floor by the fire. It was sometime during the first long night we spent together.

"You could sit and read this one book and know

everything about the entire operating environment," I said. "System calls. Commands. Network interface. Input devices. File system. The whole environment—in one book. I spent my life with this thing. I mean, it *was* my life for a while."

The book was a Bell Laboratories manual for UNIX Release 3.0. It measured six by nine inches, held about 500 pages. On the cover was the old Ma Bell logo and the date: June 1980. It came from the days when I stopped being a mere programmer and was first called a "software engineer." I looked on the inside cover where I'd written my name. Funny: my signature hadn't changed in all those years.

"Throw it away," said Brian. "It's ancient."

"Well, it's old but—"

"Throw it away!"

"What do you mean, throw it away? It's history. It's valuable."

Brian laughed at me. "It's trash."

"No, it's not trash. It's interesting." I held in my hand the little knowledge base that had made me an engineer. The whole curve of my life, my conception of myself, my sense that I could go deeper into the technical—all that came after I read that small white-covered book. How could it be trash, and so soon? I had a sudden vision of myself as a doddering codger showing off the stamp collection to junior. "It's worth looking at again," I protested. "I mean, don't you think it's bizarre that now I could fill this room with manuals, read every one of them, and still not understand the UNIX operating environment? Don't you think it means something about what's happening to our profession?"

"It's useless. Throw it away."

I didn't want my experience to be useless. I wanted it to be of value that someone could remember the lovely compactness of Release 3.0. I didn't dare show Brian my collection of manuals for ANSI-Standard COBOL, Z-80 and 8080 assembly language, System 370 Job Control Language, standard FORTRAN ("a problem solving approach"), and a 1979 Pick operating system implementation called "Reality." He would see it all as landfill, fit companions to my long disposed-of Kaypro II personal computer, first letter-quality daisy-wheel printer, and 300-baud modem with acoustic coupler.* But all this history had to be worth something, I felt. There had to be some threads, some concepts, some themes that transcended the details, something in computing that made it worth being alive for more than thirty-five years.

*The tools, languages, and hardware listed above date from the mid-1960s to approximately 1983. COBOL was the standard business-programming language during that period; it is still in use, though slowly dwindling. The Z-80 and 8080 were the standard chips on personal computers of the early 1980s. System 370 Job Control Language was used on mainframe computers that were state-of-the-art in the late 1970s. FORTRAN was one of the earliest programming languages, though it is still in use for some specialized technical applications. Pick was an operating system for minicomputers of the mid-1970s and early-1980s; it still runs on some mid-range computers but mainly as a way to keep old programs from having to be rewritten. The Kaypro computer, daisy-wheel printer, and 300-baud acoustic-coupler modem are all completely obsolete, though some survivors may still be operating somewhere.

"Okay," said Brian, finally. "The cover is history. Tear off the cover and frame it. But throw the rest away."

I put the book back on the shelf. I changed the subject. A few hours later, we were in bed. Exploratory sex: province of youth, place of forgetfulness.

Old: we don't know what to do with the word. We throw away old hardware. Old programmers are supposed to give way to twenty-year-olds. The new is what we desire, and the newer yet.

Only software gets to age. Too much time is invested in it, too much time will be needed to replace it. So, unlike the tossed-out hardware, software is tinkered with. It is mended and fixed, patched and reused. Software is almost homey, our approach to it almost housewifely. We say it has a "life cycle": from birth, to productive maturity, to bug-filled old age.

I once worked on a mainframe computer system where the fan-folded listing of my COBOL program stood as high as a person. My program was sixteen years old when I inherited it. According to the library logs, ninety-six programmers had worked on it before I had. I spent a year wandering its subroutines and service modules, but there were still mysterious places I did not dare touch. There were bugs on this system no one had been able to fix for ten years. There were sections where adding a single line of code created odd and puzzling outcomes programmers call "side effects": bugs that come not directly from the added code but from some later, unknown permutation further down in the process. My program was near the end of its "life cycle." It was close to death.

Yet the system could not be thrown away. By the time a computer system becomes old, no one completely understands it. A system made out of old junky technology becomes, paradoxically, precious. It is kept running but as if in a velvet box: open it carefully, just look, don't touch.

The preciousness of an old system is axiomatic. The longer the system has been running, the greater the number of programmers who have worked on it, the less any one person understands it. As years pass and untold numbers of programmers and analysts come and go, the system takes on a life of its own. It runs. That is its claim to existence: it does useful work. However badly, however buggy, however obsolete—it runs. And no one individual completely understands how. Its very functioning demands we stop treating it as some mechanism we've created like, say, a toaster, and start to recognize it as a being with a life of its own. We have little choice anyway: we no longer control it. We have two choices: respect it or kill it.

Old systems have a name. They are called "legacy systems." In the regular world, "legacy" has an aura of beneficence. Parents leave a child a legacy: fortunate child. A brother gets into a fraternity because of his older brother's earlier membership: a legacy admission. A gift. An enrichment. The patina of age, but *good* age—venerability, the passing on from generation to generation. A gift of time.

In computing, however, "legacy" is a curse. A legacy system is a lingering piece of old junk that no one has yet figured out how to throw away. It's something to be lived with and suffered. The system is unmodifiable, full of bugs, no longer understood. We say it's "brain dead." Yet it lives. Yet it runs. Drain on our time and money. Vampire of our happiness. *Legacy*.

In early 1980, I interviewed for a job with a man who had made his peace with his own obsolescence. He was the Information Systems manager of a large financial-services company. "I suppose you already know about our ancient system," is how he introduced himself to me.

His system was written in something called 1401 Autocoder. Before the moment I met him, I had never even heard of 1401 Autocoder. It was something older than COBOL, older than BASIC, said the manager, a tall, weary-looking man who was probably forty-five. At the time, he looked quite old to me. I was thirty-one.

The interview was brief. I knew the job was mine, if I wanted it.

Near the end of the interview, the manager lit a cigarette—this was back in the days when people still smoked—and offered me the pack. I never smoked at interviews, but the eyes looking back were deeply sad. I took a cigarette.

"Yeah. It's hard to find bright people who'll work on this thing," he said, sliding the ashtray between us.

"Uhmm," I said.

"I'd pay any amount of money. You'd have a department working for you."

"I don't know," I said, "1401 Autocoder. I've never used it."

"You'll learn. I mean, you could if you wanted to."

We smoked.

I was supposed to say I wanted to. He was practically begging me to say it. And it was a rule for me in interviews: always pretend to want the job. Still. A system before COBOL.

I didn't have to say anything. He knew: I would not take this job. He also knew it was time to end the interview. But I could tell he wanted me to stay just a bit longer. There was some camaraderie he felt with me, some confidence he was going to share. We smoked, and finally he went on: "The system's become something of, I don't know, a point of honor for me."

"Honor?" I asked.

He leaned forward and squinted at me through a veil of smoke. "I am going to be the last human being on earth who knows how to program in 1401 Autocoder."

He said this with the grim and pointless determination of a man setting off for the South Pole on foot. He encouraged me to consider joining him. There was a perverse dignity in knowing obsolete arcana, he insisted.

But he knew it was hopeless. We stubbed out our

cigarettes, he shook my hand, and he wished me good luck.

"Good luck," I echoed.

When I was at the doorway, he called out, "You're younger than I am. You'd outlive me. You could be the one: the oldest living programmer of 1401 Autocoder. Think about it!"

On a rainy Sunday afternoon, a waiter is serving me a half bottle of Pauillac, my second. "I had this wine on my twenty-fifth birthday," says the waiter, "It's good."

I stare at him for a few seconds. He's good-looking, in a wan, pony-tailed sort of way. "That was three years ago, right?" I say. I am right, perfectly. I am very good with men's ages, for some reason. But, now in middle age myself, I have trouble with women, perhaps because I don't know how old I look anymore. I look at the young and wonder, Do I still look like you?; at the old, thinking, Not yet. I don't yet look like you.

"Okay. How old am I?" I ask him. He's disconcerted for a moment; he's my waiter, after all. "No, no. Don't be polite," I say, "Be accurate. How old am I?"

He leans over and peers down at me. I feel as if every wrinkle, every mark of time, is under a cold white light.

"Forty-six," he says.

"Very good!" I say, for exactly one microsecond truly appreciating our mutual ability to guess ages, as if we could team up and get jobs as carneys at state fairs.

But I can't take this in. I want the conversation to move on. "And the women next to us," I say, "how old are they?" I had been looking at them, wondering if I were there yet.

He looks. "They're in their fifties," he says. For a moment I feel relief: I look younger, Oh good, I'm not there yet. But I can't erase the sound of the word "fifties"—the tone, the mild disdain, the dismissal, as if those women had crossed over into another reality, so that I can't for long glow in the knowledge that I look younger than they do. *In their fifties:* it speaks volumes of resignation, another country, a depressed, uninteresting region where older women are supposed to go.

And, by the reckoning of my twenty-eight-year-old waiter on a rainy Sunday afternoon, I am four years away from them, a blink by my stars, what amounts to two new operating systems and three new languages, practically no time at all. All in a day's work from here to that dull country where nothing interesting is ever supposed to happen to me again.

[6]

When the AIDS project ended, the program-
mers went away. Joel and his electric mind went back to a
contract at a hospital. Bill the network guy broke up with
his girlfriend, and, after we had a couple of talks in a café,
I lost track of him. Mark would probably come back to
work with me on another database project—this was our
second time together—but we soon stopped returning
each other's calls. Danny the desktop programmer completely disappeared from my existence. The user support
guy hired by my client had some sort of personal crisis.
He stopped working, moved, and never gave me his new
phone number; I had no use for it anyway.

Now all that was left to do was clean up the office.
I had been through it before, the closing rituals designed
to ease my way out of a project, and I dutifully went
through it all again. I sent out my final invoice. I repro-
grammed the autodial buttons on the telephone. I took
down the contact list from over the desk. I sorted through
the paper files, put them in a box, and carried them down

to the storeroom. I backed up the computer files. Then I purged them from my system.

But nothing ends all at once. Every project leaves behind a distinctive echo: a rhythm of energy, a way of speaking, a circle of relationship. For weeks I was certain I had calls to return, meetings to attend. I had gotten used to the weekly meetings with my client, with their printed agendas; to the large task-force meetings that were like performances in a play; to the meetings with the programmers, where I had to reassure them, as if they were my children, that I loved them all the same. It doesn't matter that you tell yourself you are a consultant who will go away. You've shared your working life during a time of stress, which is a precise form of intimacy. Consulting is like any relationship: it is impossible to stay in it for any length of time if you don't come to care.

And so ending a project is like the end of any relationship. I had to let go of the arguments that kept me engaged with the director. I had to let subside the anger that always keeps you tied to someone, though you tell yourself you wish to get away. I had to stop arguing with her in my head. I had to accept that my life and the life of all those people associated with the project would not intersect anymore.

Most of all, I had to accept that I was now on my own. The place I had come to before and would come to again: alone. After two weeks of intense interaction with the programmers at the networking-software company, the true nature of my new contract became clear. I sat in my loft all day staring into my computer. I designed software. Now and then, I sent the designs to the programmers by e-mail or fax. Once or twice a week, I drove down to their office through traffic made hellish by road construction. My most intense relationship became the one with my car.

I had not anticipated this return to aloneness. Sitting in my sun-filled, 1600 square feet of architectural cool, I felt light-shocked, stunned. The sudden huge quiet unnerved me. Now I spent my days in the company of machine hum. Now I worked whenever, got dressed when I had to. Time on the face of the clock meant less and less as the weeks went by. I was all unmoored again. My company and my life had devolved to their inevitable essence: me and my machines.

For I have a virtual company. Projects come and go like images in a screen saver, lovely and vibrant, one image fading into another, a steady flow of change it does no good to try to capture. The AIDS-project instantiation of my company—Joel and Danny, Mark and Bill—had been pleasant and engaging. But they were consultants themselves (each with his own little virtual company), and it was time for them to move on. Our coherence dissolved. A new image emerged: a mature product designer who drove down to Silicon Valley twice a week in a red sports car. An odd woman who appeared out of nowhere and, after a few months, would return to nowhere. Best not to think about it too much. Best just to let the old image fade and the new one form. Then to let that new fade out as well.

Clients think I'm smart for doing business like this. I have the correct "business model," as a Captain of Industry told me. "Virtual is the only way to go for consulting," he said. "Hey, you get the skills you need when you need it. And you don't get all involved in their doctor bills."

"What do I do when they get sick?" I asked.

"Get somebody else," Industry Captain said.

My clients hire me to do a job, then dispose of me when I'm done. I hire the next level of contractors then dispose of them. Layers of virtual companies. Piles of disposables. Be smart or be landfill.

There was a time (still in living memory) when "virtual" was a free word in the English language. It meant "almost true" or "for all intents and purposes, but not completely, not *truly*." One could say, "I was virtually happy." Were you truly happy? No, you weren't, because adhering to the "virtually" was the sense of the false note, something missing, an ineffable quality of not-quite-happy. To say, then, "I have a virtual company" should mean I have a not-quite-real company, something close to the reality of a company but with some essential element missing. Other people, for instance.

The word "virtual" no longer roams freely in the English language, however. It has been captured by computers. To say "virtual" means living in the not-quite-here-ness of the machine and its software. The word retains the sense of the missing, the not real. But somehow this not-ness has become a good thing. To be ephemerally existent, to float in some indefinable plane now known as cyberspace — that's supposed to be grand. The demigods, the digerati, live there. "I have a virtual company" — good, great, grand.

In my heart, I know I'm just playing at all this business stuff until the day I have to meet a payroll. I often think of my father starting up his accounting practice during the Depression. He didn't have a virtual company. He hired guys right out of school and kept them on into their dotage. (He complained about them, but he kept them on.) He gave young men part of the business, cut them into deals. His employees were like family; I called some of them "cousin." There was something in this long-term commitment, this human putting up with one another, that I know has passed away, along with a whole generation of striving immigrant sons like my father.

Then again, maybe my father's practice was a little *too* much like a family. He had to be in control, and the young men had to grow up. In the end, the "cousins" went their own ways, the employees like sons rebelled, and, when my father reached his own dotage, they complained and they *didn't* keep him on: they pitched him out of his own company. Maybe the new way is better, I think. Maybe Industry Captain is right. Just live by your wits and expect everyone else to do the same. Carry no dead wood. Live free or die. Yeah, surely, you can only rely on yourself.

This idea of self-reliance doesn't mean we've given up entirely. We're human after all; we want our compatriots around us. But a contract or a start-up company doesn't leave much room for the sentiments. Sometimes we just have a job to do.

"We're in the middle of firing my friend," said Brian. We were on our way into a restaurant the second time I saw him. "Divorce," Brian went on. "He's really been messed up. And his work has gone to trash."

"He's really messed up and so you're going to *fire* him?" I asked.

"Yeah. He's all right with it. He agrees he's screwing up."

"But how can he possibly be all right with it?"

"Oh, he's very smart. Smart enough to know when his work is bad."

"Even so. Won't this hurt your friendship?"

He shrugged. "No. Like I said, he's all right with it."

This seemed impossible to me. Or else Brian and I had very different ideas about friendship.

"I once had a bad time with a friend I hired," I told him, "and things were never the same between us."

"Uh?"

"I felt terrible, she felt terrible. In the end, the job wasn't worth all these terrible feelings."

"Uh-huh," Brian mumbled. Then he turned abruptly and walked off a ways, literally marching away from the subject of firing friends.

So I didn't tell him how my friend had sat stonily

when I tried to tell her that I thought it was only a question of her motivation, only a problem of her time; that I was sure she could do the job if she wanted to. How I kept talking and talking, and I watched her turn my words into sharp, metallic things then withdraw into a closed, self-protective anger. "Talk to me," I'd said, but she was far away and unreachable by then.

I tried to imagine telling Brian, "She's all right with it."

There seemed to be no point in mentioning that our friendship was ended on that day, and that it sent fractures through an entire circle of old friends. So that even now, nearly two years later, we are all left with the tense mess of deciding who to invite where with whom. And all this came from a talk that took maybe half an hour: fifteen years' worth of friendship trashed over a contract.

So I let the conversation go. Besides, Brian and I were only doing what we were supposed to do. We're supposed to assemble a group of people to do a job, get it done, then disassemble. We're not supposed to invest in any one person or set of skills—no sense in it anyway, as Industry Captain understood. The skill-set changes before the person possibly can, so it's always simpler just to change the person. Take out a component, put in a zippier one. The postmodern company as PC—a shell, a plastic cabinet. Let the people come and go; plug them in, then pull them out.

The day after I saw Brian, I had time to wonder why he had even brought up the subject of firing his friend.

Why tell me about it only to drop it immediately? Then I reviewed the course of the conversation and regretted I had kept my thoughts to myself. I had missed an opportunity, I thought. Maybe if I'd said something, we could have talked about it: how we're both uneasy with the way we're supposed to live. And how we do it anyway.

Living a virtual life is an art. Like all arts, virtuality is neither consistent nor reliable. It takes a certain firmness of will, and a measure of inspiration, to get up each and every day and make up your existence from scratch. As every artist knows, every writer and homebound mother, if you are not careful, your day — without boundaries as it is — can just leak away. Sundown can find all your efforts puddled around you, everything underway, nothing accomplished.

But the virtual life of techno-business requires something even more than inspiration. What is mandatory is that you present to the world the appearance of actual existence. You must seem to be a company in the usual sense of the word, with an office full of humming enterprise. Nothing is stranger than sitting in dirty sweatpants and picking up the ringing phone to say "Ellen Ullman speaking" in a mature, efficient voice. It is as if I have projected myself into another universe, where I am dressed in a blazer and slacks and my hair is washed, some place completely discontinuous with the universe I inhabit in sweats. While I speak on the phone — to a client, a

CEO—I am aware that I have thrown my voice correctly, that they have *seen* me as I wished to be seen: a clever, enterprising woman in a cool, brick-walled loft. To hang up then is almost painful. Click. I return to myself: creature swimming alone in puddles of time.

Beyond a certain tone of voice, the facade of constructed reality is entirely electronic—and therefore revirtualized. Internet address with your company name as the domain; fax machine with your company's name entered to appear on the receiving end; voice mail that answers in a receptionist-sounding voice, not your own; phone number that ends in zero-something, so that callers will believe they have reached you on your direct line, not your only line; letterheads produced on the LaserJet; invoices created by Excel or Quattro Pro or QuickBooks—all this and more create the necessary illusion of definitive, standard existence. It's a little scary just how easy it is to do this.

And, once your own electronic existence is established, you start to notice how many of the entities around you are similarly electronic and therefore as suspect in their reality as you are. Spotting other home and small businesses becomes so easy it's no sport. But what about the larger business world? Looked at in a certain way, you can ask, What is Charles Schwab but a giant computer connected to a telephone? All those buildings are there for reassurance, like the marble pillars of banks and the brick walls in my loft.

And what is a corporation these days but an elaborate verisimilitude spun round with the gauzy skin of electrics? I call an 800 number to order equipment: Am I calling the real company? Who can tell? The person I'm talking to is most likely an employee of yet another company, one that has been subcontracted to perform tele-marketing or distribution. Or, more likely yet, the individual is an independent contractor paid by the hour by the company working under contract to the company selling the equipment. And, in endless rounds of decon-struction, the company selling the equipment may itself simply be an entity with an 800 number, suppliers, and subcontractors. It orders bits of hardware from other com-panies (each with its own 800 numbers and subcontrac-tors), assembles things in cases, puts them in boxes, advertises, and lets someone else answer the phone. Behold: the modern global corporation.

And businesses that exist as Web sites: the perfect devolution. Maybe all enterprise will soon be like the NASDAQ—a network entity, wires and cables and satel-lites, everywhere available and nowhere present.

But what difference does it make: Why should I care about a company's physical coordinates? What does it matter if the person I'm talking to is sitting in the base-ment of corporate headquarters or at home thousands of miles away? The telephone, the fax, the computer net-work reach everywhere, don't they?

In the days before ubiquitous computers, I briefly worked for an insurance company. I was a temp. My job was to answer the phone in the claims department, find the claim file corresponding to the caller's auto accident (it was a paper file), put the file in a special out basket, then buzz the adjuster. Done; next call: a real shit job. The only thing that made it tolerable was the fact that, about thirty percent of the time, the file I needed was missing. This great tragedy—the lost file, motive and justification for the very existence of the business computer—was my occasion to search the premises. I went up and down the elevators, from desk to desk, learning and following the route of information inside the company. By the fifth lost file, I knew what an adjuster was, had met them all, knew what account managers did, and had met them all. I knew the full range of actions performed by an insurance company, something I'd known absolutely nothing about when I'd started. If I had wanted a career in insurance (a very unlikely ambition for me but a perfectly reasonable one for a young person with no better prospects), I was ready to advance from temporary claims-phone-answerer-file-puller to something better. At minimum, I'd like to think that the poor sufferers of automobile accidents received better service for my knowing the adjuster handling their claim—knowing him in person, by name, by looks, and by sight, by the names of his children and wife.

Twenty-five years later, the young man taking my order on the telephone was very sorry: he could not tell me if the Insert key was right next to the Backspace. This detail about a laptop's keyboard was important to me; I hate hitting Insert when I'm going for Backspace. "It's not in my database," he explained.

His name was Marshall Schoen—my experience at the insurance company made me keep up this antique tradition of asking for someone's full name. "Marshall," I said, "Is there someone you can call and ask?"

I heard him shuffling papers, hitting keys. "Sorry," he said for the second time, "All I have is the information on the screen."

"Where are you, Marshall?" I asked.

"Where? I'm. . . . What do you mean, where am I?"

"I mean physically. In what state are you, what city?"

He named a place on the prairies, fifteen thousand miles from Japan, where my prospective laptop, with its mysterious keyboard, had been designed and assembled. I felt sorry for Marshall Schoen. There he sat in his cubicle. He could not get up and hunt around for the missing information; he wasn't allowed to get up at all. All he knew was on his screen, tiny porthole surrounded by darkness. He would never learn anything about the company in Japan, about laptop computers, about the local distributor, even about the process of telemarketing. There would be no better job at this company than the one he had right now: sitting at a computer monitor, wearing a headset, answering the phone. He could stay or leave. His computer was up or down. Between those poles was nothing: no lost files and no way to find them.

"Sorry, Marshall, but I'm afraid I can't buy the laptop without knowing about the keyboard," I said, wishing I could give him the order.

I think he heard the regret in my voice. "Yeah, I see that," he said. He paused; the line went quiet, the whole global network lying between us in a vast, amazing silence. "I'm sorry, too," he said.

I used to have an idea of myself seated at a desk. I would see myself from the back, my head bent over some work, wholly absorbed in whatever I was doing. That absorption, a certain absence from one set of things and extreme presence to another, became an emblem for me, some ideal way of being, a self toward which I worked for most of my life.

It wasn't until I began to work at home, and one day during a period of anxiety mixed with boredom I projected myself across the room, so that I saw myself from the back, so to speak—it was on that day I understood that the person I had been imagining all those years was not me at all. It was instead my father, at home, at his desk, wholly absorbed in whatever he was doing.

My father had an office at home as well as his business office, and he liked to sit at his desk in the family room while my mother, sister, and I idly watched television. His ears were always covered with the headphones for his radio, which was tuned to some station playing inoffensive music. The station sounded distantly on speakers in the living room, so that I had this idea of my father as existing not here, in the family room with us, but projected into the living room, where he lived in some exalted state of busy aloneness.

It's not surprising to me, then, that I now live alone and have my office in one corner of the one large space that makes up my loft; not surprising to me that I believe I should be working all the time; no surprise at all that I can't relax except after a long bout of work. My father was presented to us as a model human being, and he was always working. But what I am surprised to learn is this: how much he wanted the isolation of work, and how much I don't.

My work hours have leaked into all parts of the day and week. Eight in the morning, ten at night, Saturday at noon, Sundays: I am never not working. Even when I'm not actually doing something that could be called work, I might get started any minute. So everything is an interruption—a call from a friend, an invitation to lunch—everything must be refused because it is possible that from one moment to the next I will get back to something.

This state of boundarylessness I could only have learned from my father. He puttered at his desk in the morning then went to the office to work; he came home, had a nap and dinner, then went to his desk in the family room to work. So it was that he was there and not there, among us and not among us, all due to the perfect protection from other human beings called having your own business.

I grew up helping my father balance his books. We did this once a month at the dining room table, with my father calling out the amounts and me totaling them on a huge, ancient adding machine. The table filled with curls of adding-machine paper. My mother brought us snacks and iced drinks on coasters. The household hushed around us.

In the end, though, this hallowed cocoon of work did no good for either me or my father. When my father feuded with his partners, he had no one to turn to, no friends, no business associates, no one but the family. But, by that time, I was as resentful as I was flattered by his attentions. More than thirty years had passed since I had helped him balance his books, years my father and I had spent admiring each other, and testing wills against each other, from a great distance. By then, we were both too attached to our working selves and had quite forgotten the language of relation. He was sick with cancer and spent his days in stunned rage over the loss of his company. Even so, it took a great deal for me to say, "I love you, Dad," and for him to answer, "The same from me."

I can see myself from the back now: at my two desks, surrounded by my four computers. I've turned on the television, a familiar noise to help me concentrate. Now and then, I'm aware that I've tuned into Ricki Lake, a program I watched for the first time when my father was dying in the hospital. What drifts back at me is the horrible boredom of death, which no one ever talks about, but which exists all the same: the hours spent sitting on a hard plastic chair in a tiny hospital room while the television, ignored by the dying, plays on for those attending. For a moment, the boredom of death and the dullness of work intersect. Am I earning a living, I wonder, or just trying to fill a very large, self-made solitude?

I'm far from unique in my lonely virtuality, I realize. The building I live in—reconstructed lofts, a kind of yuppie dorm without dining room (too bad about the dining room; food service would have made this place close to perfect)—is full of little one- and two-person companies. I'm told we home-based businesses are the new engine of employment, the future of work. Delivery guys love us: We're the new housewives. We're always home.

There is a comfort in living among one's own kind. On my way in from the garage, I pass a small loft occupied by a single man who must be in his late thirties or early forties. From his outgoing nature, I assume he is in sales—acting as a small distribution office, maybe, or a local representative of some company far away. Anyone can look in and see his clothes strewn across the floor. The man himself sits at his dining room table working on a laptop. The TV is on, ignored, for company.

In the afternoons, I see us virtuals emerge blinking into the sunlight. In the dead hours after 3 PM, we haunt cafés and local restaurants. We run into each other at the FedEx drop-box or the copy shop. They, like me, have a freshly laundered look, just come out of pajamas or sweat pants, just showered and dressed.

I recognize my virtual colleagues by their overattention to little interactions with waiters and cashiers, a supersensitivity that has come from too much time spent alone. We've been in a machine-mediated world—computers and e-mail, phones and faxes—and suddenly we're in a world where people lumber up and down the steps of buses, walk in and out of stores, have actual in-person conversations. *All this has been going on while I was in another universe:* that's what comes to us with a force like the too-bright sun or a stiff wind off the bay. We do our business, drop off the overnight packet, clip together the xeroxes, and hurry home.

Sometimes I think about taking a real job, with a real company. So what if my virtual company in its trendy loft is what everyone imagines is a perfect life? I'm no different from anyone else: I want the security, routine, and camaraderie of the office. At the AIDS project, I watched a year and a half pass in the comforting round of holidays. One day there were spiders hanging from the ceiling and witches on the wall; the next, Indian corn and leaves pinned to the windows, like a grade-school classroom in the coziness of fall; later, blinking lights on the reception desk, the tree, the holiday party. I think it would be relaxing to take a job, have the soothing circle of the seasons go 'round you, go someplace where they'll understand if you get sick or just tired.

Then I remember: I was once a devoted employee. I stayed at a software company for two years, left, went back. Contented in that real-company sort of way, I thought I would stay forever.

But one day I arrived late to work from a dentist's appointment to find my colleagues heading toward me with their belongings in cardboard boxes. The software company had been swallowed up by a much larger one. Only a small maintenance crew would be left. My project and all the others had been killed, and what remained of two years of my group's work was on a computer tape someone made in a hurry. Later, it turned out that the tape was unreadable.

Of the original project team—something grandly called "The Advanced Products Group"—only my boss and I were left. We were now to be in charge of "special projects." That is, we'd been given the courtesy of time to look for new work.

Soon a work crew came to take down the partitions. Until then, for the first day or two after the layoff, it hadn't been clear how alone my boss and I were. Once the cubicles came down, though, we could see all the empty desks. We could see how packed in we all had been—a vast space that once had been filled with programmers. After the partitions, the next things to go were workstations and monitors. Then the freestanding furniture. Last were the phones. In the end, we were left with a whole office floor with nothing but carpeting and dangling cables. Falling from ceiling tiles, cascading from posts, dripping down walls— nothing but the sprung ends of dead computer networks.

It was all the dangling cable that finally drove us out. My boss and I had been huddling near our former work-spaces—what once had been "deluxe" cubicles, the double-wides of the modular office-furniture world. But there was something about all the open space and cabling. We strolled around and around the empty space for two days, wondering what we should do. To pass the time, we counted the number of dead connectors: how many RJ11s, serials, parallels, phone jacks. Once we had counted all the cables, we gave up. We withdrew to the last two solid offices: things with hard walls, metal windows, wooden doors. From there, we used the last remaining phone to start the search for new work.

My boss and I never really spoke about it, but over the years, in odd indirect ways, we've signaled to each other how we went to opposite and extreme reactions against all that emptiness, all those sprung dead cables. No one who goes through a layoff is ever the same again. Some faith is gone, some comfort level is lost. You learn how delicate your place in the world is. Any day, you could be coming from the dentist to find that your social, laboring existence has literally been ripped away.

For me, the layoff started a time of wandering. I went to a start-up company, then on to my virtual, consulting ways. My boss took a job with a computing research group at Pacific Bell—a big company, a solid company. The *phone company,* for heaven's sake, bound to be around forever, right?

Twelve years after my former boss took his job at the phone company, a major telecommunications deregulation bill became law. Layoffs are occurring everywhere in the telephone industry. AT&T has already shed tens of thousands of workers, and Pacific Bell is being acquired. I've begun to worry about my former boss: twelve years on the job, and what will happen to him now?

And then here I am, rootless and wandering, my company wavering in and out of existence. I used to think that I was the infantile one, that I couldn't accept reality like my former boss and just settle down. But now I feel he will be more fragile. Unprepared for chaos, he must go out into the hurly-burly I've been in all these years. In the end, which of us is better prepared for the world as it has turned out to be?

I'm bad at letting go. Even after projects end and I should let associates fade out, I try to hold on, sometimes to a fault. I was not ready to let go of Joel, for example. We had shared minds that night before the AIDS-project release, and mind-share, for me, is the hardest bond of all to break.

Joel and I met for dinners. It turned out we both had a passion for good wine and fancy restaurants. I liked that he would appear in a suit and tie, his good-biz-school self fitting right into the sort of places I like to go to.

One night we met at a restaurant near my loft. It was down a little alley, behind a gate. Our confirmed reservation, and Joel's good suit and overcoat, got us past the crowd at the door and into the inner dining room, where we were seated at a table with softly upholstered chairs. The room was filled with flowers, huge vases with three-foot stems and blossoms inches in diameter.

We chose the food and the wine—planning our orders as a single meal—and soon turned to the subject that occupied the largest part of our lives: work. That night, Joel had a complaint. In the face of new government regulations, the company where he had been a contractor for years was talking about forcing him to become something terrible: an employee.

"Why does the government give a damn what I am?" said Joel. "If the company is happy and I'm happy, why should it be any of their business?"

"Joel, it's the government's business because contracting is so often abused."

"What do you mean? What's the difference? If you want to work for yourself, why should anybody stop you?"

"*You* want to work for yourself. But what about someone who doesn't want to?"

Joel looked at me with utter incomprehension. "Why would someone not want to work for himself?"

Joel wasn't a proper libertarian; his individualism wasn't studied and rationalized like Brian's. But he was the same age as Brian, thirty-one, and I decided that their obliviousness toward the average working life had to be some by-product of their age and time. They didn't want to make films or write novels, the way my friends did at thirty. They wanted to build companies, be in charge, on their own. Somehow, having your own business had become cool.

"Benefits," I said. "That's why people want jobs. And companies don't pay benefits to contractors." He still didn't quite get it. "Don't they teach labor history in school anymore?"

I had to explain that companies would make everyone a contractor if there weren't laws against it; that they would jump at the chance to unload the cost of medical coverage, overtime, holidays, sick leave.

"You think so?"

"Jesus, Joel. Companies don't give benefits because they like to. People had to die in the streets—literally—to get these benefits."

"Did they?" Suddenly he seemed suspicious of me. Maybe I was indeed a decently successful software developer. Maybe I did read *The Economist*. Maybe we did get along quite well in nice restaurants. But there I was talking dead people in the street, just like some sort of commie.

We sat in the beautiful restaurant. Before us was a bottle of old, red wine. The vases of fresh cut flowers surrounded us. I lifted my glass. I talked labor history of the '20s. For the five-day work week, people did indeed get shot by company thugs and die in the streets; and there we sat, two independent contractors who brag about working all the time. Virtual employer and virtual employee, sipping their wine.

Finally Joel just gave up. "Whatever. I'm sure you're right. I mean, I take your word for it."

I had a vision of my so-right self sitting behind the remains of my *gigot en chevreuil*. "Oh, please don't take my word for it, Joel. These days I'm liable to say just about anything."

The dining room began to empty. The ghost scents of food, flowers, and coffee rose around us. We finished the bottle. We shared a dessert. When we left the table, I instinctively brushed my arm around him, and he circled my waist. Zing. Rush. How strange: that mind-moment we had shared on our long night of programming, that little thought-charge—it was still there.

I decided that Joel could live without a real job because he had a fake one: he was an "independent" contractor who had a whole little society to live in. Every day for years, he went to an office and sat at the same desk in the same cubicle. The same people were there to say good morning and how are you and did you see a certain movie. There was someone to eat lunch with and chat with and help pass bored time. When things went wrong, he had a companionable ear for gossip and complaint.

He had his home in the postmodern village: the workplace, the last place where your position in the order of things is still known, where people must put up with you on a regular basis, over a long period of time, and you with them. Families scatter, marriages end, yet the office and the factory have hung on a bit longer as staple human gathering places. Maybe this is why the decline of industrial work and the downsizing of corporations have produced such anxiety: the final village is dissolving, and those of us without real jobs or fakes—where will we meet each other now?

On line, I suppose. As virtualized creatures swimming alone in private pools of time.

In this sense, we virtual workers are everyone's future. We wander from job to job, and now it's hard for anyone to stay put anymore. Our job commitments are contractual, contingent, impermanent, and this model of insecure life is spreading outward from us. I may be wrong, but I have this idea that we programmers are the world's canaries. We spend our time alone in front of monitors; now look up at any office building, look into living-room windows at night: so many people sitting alone in front of monitors. We lead machine-centered lives; now everyone's life is full of automated tellers, portable phones, pagers, keyboards, mice. We live in a contest of the fittest, where the most knowledgeable and skillful win and the rest are discarded; and this is the working life that waits for everybody. Everyone agrees: be a knowledge worker or be left behind. Technical people, consultants, contract programmers: we are going first. We fly down and down, closer and closer to the virtualized life, and where we go the world is following.*

---

*Companies are shedding employees then regaining the use of their labor as "contingent workers": as on-call workers, temporaries, workers provided by contract firms, and independent contractors. According to a labor department study cited in the *New York Times* (December 8, 1996), 17 percent of all contingent workers had a previous relationship with the company at which they were working. Over 22 percent of independent contractors had such a previous relationship. A temporary-help agency that supplies contract workers to Pacific Bell said that, on an average day, former employees represent 80 percent of the people they place at the phone company.

While I was still on the AIDS project, I took my virtual company out to lunch. Danny the desktop programmer, Mark on the server, Bill the network specialist, the user support guy, me. (Joel hadn't started working with us yet.) To celebrate making our first major project milestone, we drank some very nice Veuve Clicquot, ate an excellent meal at my expense, praised each other, teased one another, and generally had a fine time. But, even with two excellent bottles of wine after the champagne, we knew to hold back. We were careful not to say too much about ourselves, careful not to make assumptions about the future. We were all practiced virtuals. We knew better than to get involved.

After the lunch, I went home to my office. The floor was covered with boxes, new hardware to be installed. As I snaked cables under desks, I thought about how I would eventually lose touch with the guys who'd been so funny that day over the pasta, and how the hardware I was cabling, soon to be wired and communicating, would stay.

I had a rush of affection for the machines. They had a presence, a solidity, that made the empty office feel occupied. On the network, each one had a name. I called them Janeway and HomePlanet, Pride and Hubris. In the virtual company, these were my real companions. They'd be here for me when others moved on. When they got sick, though, I could junk them without regrets. When they got old, I'd just scrap them. Why bother messing up good friendships? What's the point of all these people coming and going in your life? And who needs to work with family anyway? Your good pals could just as well pitch you out of your own company someday. I was a bit woozy, I realized. Too much champagne in the afternoon. "You machines will be obsolete long before I will," I said aloud with stupid bravado.

The machines didn't say anything, of course. Janeway beeped when she came up. HomePlanet had a boot error. Pride and Hubris—they just sat there.

[7]

One day, the Ping-Pong table disappeared. I arrived for a meeting at the networking-software company, and the only evidence that there ever was a Ping-Pong table was a crumpled ball hiding in the corner. In its place were cubicles: a row of four cubes along the window, four more facing them across a newly invented narrow corridor, ten more stretching down toward the hallway, even one in the corner of the large room where the programmers usually did technical design, and which was now strewn with half-assembled equipment.

"Where is everybody?" I asked the first person to come along, someone I didn't recognize. He waved vaguely at the cubicles. "Oh, I don't know. Just look around."

The offices that had been vacant were now full of strange people. "Isn't this Steve's office?" I asked a heavy-set man sitting in what used to be the product manager's office. "Oh, Steve's in one of the cubicles," said the man. He seemed harried and not inclined to introduce himself.

"And you are. . . ?" I asked him. "From upstairs," he said, "Sales." Again he ignored me, clearly wishing I'd just go away. But where were all the missing people?

"Is everyone who was in an office—"

"Is in a cubicle," he said.

"And everyone now in an office—"

"Is from sales, marketing, finance. Everyone from upstairs and across the hall."

"What happened, I mean—"

"We're consolidating," he said, "Anyway, I have to make a call, so. . . ." He shut the door behind me.

I went back to the receptionist and asked after the senior engineer and product manager I was supposed to meet with. "They're not in today," said the receptionist, who was also new to me.

"Are you sure?" I said, "We had a meeting scheduled for—"

"Sorry. They're not in."

She smiled in a way that told me I wouldn't get any explanations here. "Well then, here's my card. Please tell them—"

"Of course," she said.

There was nothing for me to do but start the long drive back north to the city. I spent two hours in creeping traffic. I vowed to bill the company for the entire day.

This happened on a Friday, after which I went away for the weekend. I enjoyed myself and nearly stopped thinking about the bizarre state of affairs at the networking-software company. Then, when I checked my messages on Sunday night, there was a call on my work line which had come in on Friday night. It was from the representative of the venture capitalists, the salvage specialist who had hired me.

"I'm going on vacation Monday," said the message, "so give me a call before then. I should be here until midnight, same on Saturday." Then he left his home and cell phone numbers and repeated the instructions to call him. *Uh-oh,* I thought. No one calls at ten on Friday and asks for a call back until midnight, unless he has something bad to say.

I left messages for him on Monday, Tuesday, and Wednesday. No calls back. Finally, on Thursday, there was an answer on his cell phone.

"Hey, there!" said the salvage specialist, a former Navy frigate commander who sounded exactly like that. "Greetings from Death Valley!"

"Is that where you are, Death Valley?"

"Yes, indeed. Here with the family. And the weather is hot and fine. We're camping. You should see it: we're out in the middle of nowhere."

I imagined him standing in the middle of the desert with a cell phone to his ear. "I'm very sorry to disturb you on vacation but—"

"No problem! No problem!" he said in such good spirits that I wondered if I had been wrong about the bad news.

"Well, things have gotten very strange down in San Jose, and I was wondering if—"

"I could explain? Hey, that's why I called you!" he said, again in expansive spirits.

But his good mood must have come from the vacation; the story he had to tell was dismal enough. The venture capitalists had based their last two rounds of financing on the hiring of a new company president. The new president, a short, slight man of about forty, had come aboard, hired his buddies, started opening an office close to his home then—in less than a month—he quit.

"That was fast," I said.

"Well, he and we had different ideas about the company's future."

With the departure of the president and his team, the venture capitalists were reconsidering their investment. They were not going to fund another round just yet. The interim vice president had two weeks to come up with a plan that would get the company to the first release of the product I was working on—without any additional funding.

"What are the chances of that succeeding?" I asked.

"Well, I wouldn't write this thing off just yet," he said, but he sounded dubious.

"So much for stock options," I said.

"You're not the only one," he said.

"And should I continue to—"

"No. Better stop working and see what happens."

It took a moment for this news to sink in: I could be out of a job. This sudden unemployment made me think of my two outstanding invoices. "I hate to seem self-serving at a time like this," I said, "but do you think I'll get paid?"

"Oh. Don't worry," he said, again in his hale, frigate-commander voice, "We are very good about things like this. We always do an orderly shutdown."

"I'll get paid?"

"Orderly shutdown. As I said, we're very good at things like that."

I had forgotten that start-up companies could fail. Like the rest of the world, I had let myself become intoxicated by Silicon Valley's aura of high-tech riches. I had started thinking of my stock options in multiples of ten dollars, which I thought of as their minimum price at the initial public offering. Two companies I'd worked for had gone public, so perhaps I can be forgiven my unthinking sense of entitlement.

Before any of this happened—before I had experienced the heady fright of watching a company go public—I imagined that the options or certificates I held would make great bathroom decorations. I even had some proper frames. I looked forward to the cool cachet of having worthless stock hanging over the towel rack.

Then came the first IPO, then the second. Both began with letters from lawyers reminding everyone of the rules: the certificates had to be registered, you can't sell for six months from the date of the initial public offering. It's then strange that no official letters come from the lawyers on the actual date. It's only when someone calls—breathless, giggling; the most staid antimaterialist you know suddenly gibbering at the thought of riches—it's then you realize that the impossible has truly happened. Your stock is not toilet paper.

Now come the awful six months of waiting. The stock price is sickeningly volatile. The underwriters push the stock: it goes up. A quarterly report comes out: it goes down. Programmers suddenly become technical analysts. They order newsletters. They open accounts at Charles Schwab. They chart the stock and plan their "sell targets."

Not everyone becomes fabulously wealthy, of course. I left before I had vested all my options. My stock earnings were enough for a sweet, fast sports car and a good-sized down payment on a loft, for which I am immensely grateful. It is an extraordinary thing to be living your life more or less as you would anyway, then receive an unexpected pile of money.

I knew someone who was an early employee of Sun Microsystems. He was a shy writer of compilers* who tended to wear flannel shirts. A few years out of engineering school, he had taken a job at the then-unknown company. Eight years later, Sun was a leading technology corporation, and my friend was probably worth tens of millions of dollars.

"But why are you still working?" I asked him one day.

---

*A compiler is a computer program that translates "higher-level" languages, such as BASIC, C, or COBOL, into machine-readable code.

"Life would have no meaning if I didn't work," he said. "Besides, I *like* writing compilers."

My first start-up company began in a decrepit suite of former doctors' offices. There were six of us: the four founders, an administrative assistant, me. For offices, we each had a tiny examining room, every one with its own sink and stainless-steel examination table. On Friday nights, starting with my very first one, we had a wine-and-cheese party—this was the sort of company that had wine glasses and a corkscrew before it had staplers.

Within months, about twenty more engineers and a skeleton executive staff were hired. We moved to real offices. The entire company stopped going out to lunch together; the programmers now went with programmers, management with management. But the Friday night parties continued on schedule—after which everyone was expected to go back to work.

Soon venture capitalists began coming to the Friday night parties. Up until then, the company had been running on the founders' investments, which would not last us much longer. The first night the VCs appeared, they emerged loose-tied and jacketless from a closed-door meeting that had gone on all day. They made their way to the table, staying bunched up among themselves. The administrative assistant poured them wine and served them food.

One VC proposed a toast. "Work hard!" he exclaimed.

Another raised his glass. "Work long hours!" he said.

The programmers looked surprised but drank down. "Make us a lot of money," I murmured under my breath.

For in those days I had a low view of these venture capitalists. I wondered why they didn't circulate among us and find out who we were. What else were they buying but the intelligence of fifteen engineers? Experienced managers and a good business plan weren't going to get very far without some programming talent. Later, I met one of them on an airplane flight. A single empty seat was between us, and we would be near each other for the next six hours. I introduced myself as a senior engineer at the company. I felt certain he would strike up a conversation with me; I was sure he would want an engineer's view of how the product was progressing. Five and three-quarter hours later, he had not said a word to me. After we landed, he waved and said, "Good luck."

In the first round of financing, the VCs gave the company two million dollars. The founders held a party to celebrate. At the party, someone took a Polaroid of the president then later pinned it to the bulletin board over the coffee pot, where it hung for months. In the picture, the president is holding the check up to the camera with both hands. The check is actually made out in the amount of two million dollars. The president is clearly drunk. On his face is a sloppy, boozy, greedy smile.

Exactly eleven years and three months later, long after I'd quit, I went back to the company. This time, I was there to meet with the new vice president of external affairs, who would see to it that Project Reggie received a generous donation of software, training, and service. The company president—the very same boozy, greedy one from the picture—had gone out of his way to arrange the donation.

I put on a good suit and real pearls. I parked the car I had bought with the company's stock. I stepped out, looked up and stopped: there before me was the very materialization of success. A corridor of palm trees. A line of black-glass buildings. A brand-new office park, head-quarters of the company I had worked for when we squatted in the vacated medical suite, each office with a sink. Stretching out to the north, more buildings holding the company's name, warehouses and offices, trucks coming and going from loading docks. Somewhere in all those buildings, and in others around the world, were thousands of employees. Fifteen of us had built the entire first product; what were all those employees doing, I wondered?

I had always imagined that wealth was something to be amassed—something that previously existed and was then accumulated, and therefore had to be taken away from someone else. I never held much truck with the libertarian idea that wealth could be created—created where there had been none. This idea of theirs seemed a self-serving dream, a salve on the conscience which permitted someone to become rich without care or guilt.

But if wealth could not be created, how else to explain all that had happened since I left the company: the line of glass-cube buildings, the spanking-new office park, the thousands of employees, the millionaire programmers, the manager I once reported to (former mailman-bartender-librarian), who was now a multimillionaire philanthropist? How to account for my car, my loft? If wealth could not arise like life out of the primordial soup, where else did it come from? How had the efforts of fifteen people gone on to become (according to the company's publicity department) "the sixth-largest independent software company in the world?"

And what was I doing to spread around the wealth? With my little virtual company expanding and contracting, never paying a salary—what was I doing? I looked back at my rebellious self who had hated the venture capitalists. Though it's difficult to like people with extraordinary amounts of money, still I had to admit: they weren't just sitting on their yachts.

The office park was deserted, except for a few delivery vans and maintenance workers. Walking by the perfect trees and clipped hedges, the few people about looked like figures in an architect's rendering. Then, something about the unreal landscaping and fake-looking people and the black-glass buildings gave me a brief, scary vision. Inside the buildings it seemed there were nothing but knowledge workers, and outside, stuck in this bizarrely perfect place, were all the people who existed to serve the knowledge-force. It was like a vision that would sometimes come to me in Manhattan: an island of very wealthy people surrounded by the people whose role in life was to take care of their children, pick up their dry cleaning, and deliver Chinese take-out. As I made my way across the parking lot and stepped into the cool entranceway, it seemed to me that I'd crossed the great divide and could not go back. I was on the inside now. I was on my way to see a vice president of the sixth-largest software company in the world.

The vice president of external affairs had described himself on the phone as "a dumb right-wing Republican," and he was a little afraid of anything to do with AIDS. It was for him that I had put on the good suit I was wearing and the real pearls, the shoes from France and my father's gold watch. After asking my way through a maze of corridors, I found his door. He looked up, saw me in my excellent clothes, and visibly relaxed. I was one of his, said the image I offered up in the doorway.

My first impulse had been to show up in black leathers—to give the dumb, right-wing Republican a good fright. The fact that I didn't: Was it all because of the stock? Did I feel obligated for what I'd been given? Had the grumbling, rebellious programmer who left behind a fortune in stock options been changed that much by her unexpected pile of money? And, if I had changed, was it a good thing or a bad one?

"You know, you were almost the food-irradiation heiress," said my father.

He made this statement to me one morning, completely out of the blue. I was in New York one winter for a visit home. We had been sitting in silence all through breakfast (my father was then in his mid-seventies, still working, on his way to the office), when he stood up, cleared the remains of his sardines and pot cheese, and started talking about food irradiation.

"Just what in the world is a food-irradiation heiress?" was the natural thing for me to ask.

My father laughed, which in him was a sort of mild cough. "Well," he said, putting the breakfast dishes in the dishwasher, "if Semi and I hadn't been so ahead of our time, you'd be on your way to inheriting an entire empire of food-preservation plants."

The story came out as the dishwasher filled. My father and his younger brother—Seymour, called Semi— had met some man who knew someone who was an engineering professor at Princeton. This man convinced my father and his brother that the future of food processing was in low-level doses of radiation, which would sterilize and preserve anything, he said. In exchange for the rights and means to develop the process of food irradiation, the brothers had invested twenty-five thousand dollars each.

"And do you know what fifty thousand dollars was in those days?" he said.

He was talking about the early sixties. "A fortune," I said.

"Ach! You don't know. We had the equipment ready, we had the building leased—this was in Connecticut— and we had a contract with the Navy. Fish."

"Fish?"

"Fish. The Navy wanted us to preserve fish. So it would last on ships."

"So what happened?"

"What happened? The people in the town heard about the whole thing and got scared. You know, radiation. It scared them. What a mess! They blocked the permit, we lost the lease, and there went your future as the food-irradiation heiress."

Looked at this way, having avoided a future where I might have poisoned, or at least terrified, an entire town in Connecticut, I was rather glad not to have become the food-irradiation heiress. But I couldn't say that. My father took any disagreement as a sign of ingratitude. He was a man who liked to give, to provide; and he liked his providees to be grateful.

"Was this around the time that you and Uncle Seymour did that thing with the coin counter?" Now that I thought of it, I remembered that my father somehow got in the business of manufacturing a plastic device for counting coins, an idea he'd gotten from watching cashiers handle money in some diners he'd invested in (one of the diners had—well—burned down). And this memory triggered another: of my father sitting at this very kitchen table trying to convince a distantly related son-in-law, a doctor, to "invent some pill to put in a ketchup bottle to make it come out faster." These moments had occurred to me in childhood as single, unconnected events. Suddenly, with the revelation of food irradiation, I realized that my apparently traditional, conservative father—who had always counseled everyone to invest safely and carefully—had himself been something of a financial wildman.

"Come to think of it, Dad, you got involved in some pretty strange things."

"Are you complaining?" He lifted his chin to me. "You had such an insecure childhood?"

I had everything, I was supposed to say. "I had everything," I said.

"Uhmm. And then some."

"And then some."

He let that hang for a minute. At one time, this would be the place where he'd bring up the trips to the toy store, later the Ivy League college I went to, later a certain relationship I had with the shoe department at Barney's. By now, though, he didn't need to say a word. A pause was enough for me to fill it in by myself.

"But the food-irradiation business—well, that was something else. Something...." He paused, looked out the window, sighed. "Oh well, too bad. Because we were going to make money in that one. A *lot* of money." Another pause. "*Real* money."

What a very odd thing for him to say: *real* money. I had never known my father to talk about money. And especially not like this: as an object of desire. In our house, we were supposed to understand that money was for security, that my father made more than enough of it, that the making of money was his sole and uncontested province, and that he ruled his province very, very well. Beyond that, the matter was not to be directly mentioned. Now, suddenly, here he was at the kitchen sink one winter morning, on his face a look of intense pleasure and regret at the memory of his (and my) lost fortune.

"Come in the den," he said, "I want to show you something."

The den—family room and office—was dark at this early hour and empty of family. My father switched on the light over the desk. "I want you to know where everything is," he said.

He opened the middle drawer and pulled out a wide, well-worn leather ledger. "This is where I record all the income," he said. It was the book I had seen him writing in all those years, or another just like it. "For example, see here? Last month. This is a list of all the partnerships and their deposits."

He ran his hand down the penciled column and recited the names of partnerships. "Gotham, Southbury, Ullman and Company, Miller and Ullman, A. Ullman and Sons, Ullman Realty, Ullman 63"—names that once rang through my childhood as echoes of my father's other life, sounds overheard during the business calls he took at the dinner table, names I understood dimly even then, with my father old and me at the entrance of middle age.

"But you know I can't read your handwriting!" My father wrote in a cramped, odd hand that looked like a collection of stick figures.

"What do you mean, you can't read my handwriting?"

"Just that: I can't. It's impossible. You know that! No one can."

"Is that so? I had a whole office full of people working for me and you're telling me no one could read my writing?" He laughed. "You'll figure it out." He was as certain as ever that I could do anything; I had been left alone most of my life to "figure it out." But about this at least he was right. When he died, his business affairs in a mess, no lawyer hired, I was the one to go through his desk and his files. I was the one to follow the trail of his money, which he had left in transit, as if he thought that, if his funds were still afloat, he could not die.

"And in this drawer are all the checkbooks—"

"But what are those back there?"

"More checkbooks."

The tour continued. "Here is where I keep deposit receipts"—a drawer with slips of paper thrown in—"and here are invoices"—a jammed file.

And so went the great unlocking of the fortress desk, promontory from which my father spent his life surveying his family and his money. Here the statements, there the canceled checks—its secrets revealed as ordinary paper, mundane matter, plain stuff. A wave of disappointment came over me: I didn't want this coming down to size, I realized; I wanted my father to remain forever a mysterious, distant figure of busy wonder. And if I were to finally know him, I wanted some extraordinary moment, a grand declaration of our stiff-necked love for each other. But immediately I was aware of the yellow cone of light circling us in the dim room. I felt the quiet of the house around us. This was my father, I saw. He was not a man for grand declarations. If I kept hoping for that, I would always be disappointed. How else could he reveal himself to me except like this: in money and papers and accounts.

I didn't know then that my father's business had started to fall apart. I wasn't aware that he had tried and failed to reach a retirement agreement with his partners, and the feud that was to drain his last years had already begun. It was only after he died that I understood what had prompted this unexpected set of revelations, why he had this sudden need to talk to someone who still thought of him as powerful, to someone like me, who was still deep down afraid of him.

"Now look in here," said my father, opening a small loose-leaf binder filled with columnar paper. "These are the accounts for the real estate, the rents and operating expenses and so forth." Again came his finger down penciled columns, again the recital of familiar names—tenants, janitors, suppliers—more echoes from the telephone.

He flipped through the pages and became pensive, as if he were remembering something or looking for something. Finally, he opened to a page where a yellowed paper was folded over and clipped.

He removed the clip, opened the paper carefully. "This is it," he said, holding the book up to me as if it were the key to all mysteries, the explanation for everything.

"This is what?"

"The spreadsheet where I figured out I could afford

to buy John Street."

John Street: Our building. Our piece of Wall Street. Our fortune, the one that did happen.

"Do you know what you're looking at? See this here? That's what I started with: ten thousand dollars." He repeated the three words individually. "*Ten . . . thousand . . . dollars.* That was it. All I had. Do you know what leveraging is? Debt! It's debt. A great big load of debt. Biggest crapshoot of my life."

Debt. Crapshoot. Had this been inside him all these years? Did all his accountant's perfect navy blue suits cover the soul of a gambler?

"It was a risky business. But it paid off. Do you know what it's worth now?" The market was yet to crash; Wall Street was yet to become unpeopled; our fortune was still intact. "Your dear father made this happen. Everything we have now started right here. Money, Ellie. *Real* money. You see, it's not the accounting business that interests me. I got bored by that years ago. It's the deals, Ellen, the *deals.*"

It was as close to a moment of passion as my father had ever shown. So here at last was what drove him. Here was what had kept him at that desk all those nights while the TV played. Here was what made him take all the phone calls at dinner. Deals: it was the deals.

Just then, for the first and last time, I saw the young man in him. I saw the ambition, the drive, the virile desire that had attracted him to the making of money — *real* money. And I saw the enormous, dominating ego that lived under the unassuming look of the prosperous accountant. There, exposed, was the stubborn force that I had sparred with—at a distance, by proxy—all my life. *Real money. I did it. I made it. The deals.* There it was: the life overheard from the wrong end of the phone, an almost dangerously determined manhood played out in the wilds of money.

"Jack!" came my mother's voice from the upstairs bedroom. "*Jack!*"

The silence around us dissolved. The enclosing dark of the room descended to ordinary day. The early morning was over: my mother was awake. "Jack! Don't tell me you're going to the office today! It's going to snow."

My father looked at me. This was the other side of his life.

"She has a point, you know," I said. "You are seventy-five, after all. Why don't you stay home with her?"

"*Jack!*" came again, insistent and annoyed.

"Yes, Mother dear," my father called out, playing the role of henpecked husband he liked to affect with my mother.

"Go ahead," I said.

And he closed the desk drawers, switched off the light, and obediently went up to her. And, after they had the usual exchange of words about this subject, he brought her coffee to her. Then he folded the business section of the *Times,* put it in his briefcase, and went to the office.

What makes a man spend his whole life making money? What makes him risk everything, forsaking hobbies, interests, friends, even family? I took the elevator up to the eighth floor of an exclusive building in Pacific Heights to ask this question of a very rich man.

The building held one apartment to a floor, and the family name — which I'll call Charles — was listed on a plaque in the elevator. I had met both Mr. and Mrs. Charles at the office party of a money-management company I'd worked for. Holding glasses of good cabernet, we had discussed his private men's club, something like the exclusive Bohemian Club but more discreet. I was amazed to find myself talking with a man who was so extremely wealthy but whom I did not immediately despise. I even enjoyed him, so much so that his wife had to come looking for him to drag him away. John Charles was an adviser to CEOs. He'd been born in Denver when it was still a mining town, and had started up companies ranging from ticket services to manufacturing. He went on to become a turnaround specialist before getting involved in the CEO-advising business. Now he was a rich man who counseled other rich men on how to become even richer: the perfect source to help me penetrate the mysterious drive to make money. I called and told him I was writing something. Could I come over and talk with him about what motivated the men he worked with? He remembered me from the party. He'd read some articles I'd written about technology companies. And he was flattered. He said yes.

The elevator opened to a small vestibule with a single door. I knocked. Mr. Charles himself opened the door.

"Thank you for seeing me," I said.

"Come in, come in," he fussed, "but I don't know how much use I'll be."

The entrance opened into a large living room, maybe forty feet long and twenty wide. The floor was old parquet. The furniture, like the building, was of another era. Crystal sconces, smoked mirrors, paneled walls and ceiling—all the fancy stuff of the twenties, that great time for the wealthy before big income taxes. I could see an adjoining dining room, entirely paneled in polished oak. Off the living room was a glassed-in porch, a protected balcony from which Mr. and Mrs. Charles could overlook the world. The city rolled away beneath us. The bay curved from northwest to southeast. Beyond were the hills of Marin. And there were the bridges: to the east the Bay Bridge; to the north the orange span of the Golden Gate.

"What a wonderful view!" I said, as Mr. Charles settled us in the porch, with its old rattan and wicker furniture. "Is the building from the twenties?"

"Exactly," said John Charles. "This apartment was originally built by a Frenchman. All the brass on the doors"—he indicated the sun-porch doors and the entrances to other rooms—"was cast in Paris and shipped to San Francisco for assembly."

John Charles was the whitest man I had ever met. Then in his late sixties or early seventies, he was trim and white-haired, his hair combed back from a still-handsome face. His shirt was unbuttoned two buttons, showing an able chest for a man his age. He looked like David Niven with a few years on him. I could easily imagine Mr. Charles on safari in Africa, posing by a kill with pith helmet and rifle. But there was no sign of big game, only the wicker furniture, which—weathered and worn in the way only very expensive things can be—might have been carried off from some place called "Raffles."

I asked about his life, about which he was circumspect, and finally got to the questions that had brought me there.

"These men you advise—what do you think drives them? It has to be more than money; they already have a lot of money. What is it—what is it inside them?"

Mr. Charles seemed confused. "Do you want me to examine their psychologies?"

"Yes. If you can. The best you can. What motivates them?"

He thought a minute. "Well, I suppose it's that they want to see their companies grow."

"But why keep growing?" I asked. "Can't someone simply enjoy a good living, a nice life?"

Mr. Charles looked away, moving his mouth in a gesture that could only have been distaste. "It's boring," he said finally. "It's simply not interesting to do the same thing with your company year after year. I won't work with someone who doesn't want to grow."

"But many people find pleasure in other parts of life, don't they? What do you think it is about these CEOs you work with? What kind of person looks for all his satisfactions in growing a company? Any why—why do that instead of, I don't know, getting a Ph.D. or learning French?"

Again Mr. Charles looked away.

"It can't just be the money," I pressed.

"Well, it might be that they have what they think is a good idea. . . ." He trailed off then sat looking at his hands, which were fine-boned and pale.

But there are many ways to express a good idea, I thought. One could talk to people, give a speech, write an article, perhaps a book. But it was clear these were not the sort of good ideas he had in mind. No, his were the sorts of ideas whose goodness could be expressed only through the amount of revenue they generated, the size of the company that was grown, the grandeur of the CEO's house, the price of the stock.

"So it *is* the money," I said finally.

The whitest man I ever met looked into his lap then gazed out the window. On the other side of the French doors edged in bronze from Paris, the sky was the bright, deep blue of early autumn in San Francisco. The two bridges stood against a sparkling bay. The searchlight of Alcatraz blinked rhythmically against the water. Toward the northwest, a tanker was slowly sliding out the Gate, about to pass under the bridge on its long ride west to Japan.

The networking-software company lingered on for a while. After a hiatus of two weeks, I was called back to work. The idea was that, if we finished the product, the company might be easier to sell. Maybe some other venture capitalists would be willing to invest in it for a while.

The sales and finance people — the current office occupants — had a dejected and distracted air about them. They didn't have much to do except sit around and worry. Not so for the programmers. The engineers continued working their endless days and long weeks. The lead engineer went on sitting in his charged way in his cubicle, his knees opening and closing, opening and closing.

A merry kind of hysteria took over the programmers. The situation was impossible, the deadline was ridiculous, they should have been completely demoralized. But, somehow, the absurdity of it all simply released them from the reality that was so depressing the rest of the company. They played silly jokes on one another. They stayed up late to see who could finish their code first. The very impossibility of success seemed to make the process of building software only that much sweeter.

The lead engineer wanted me to come in every day to see their progress. "Look," he said, "you just select the device and drag it over to the location tree —"

"— and boom!" said another programmer, "It updates. Just like in your specs."

"And the database is updated?" I asked.

"Done!" said the lead.

"And the multiple add," said a third programmer, a young Chinese woman who looked exhausted but who was clearly having the time of her life, "look at this." She typed in a few parameters and the screen filled with information as the program cranked away.

"Does it crash?" I asked.

"Only a little," she said.

"Twice yesterday," said the second programmer.

"No," said the lead, "once. Only once!"

They arranged a demonstration of their work for the entire company. They put out cake, ice cream, champagne. The worried sales and finance people did their best to be impressed.

In the middle of the demo, I realized how fortunate we were to be engineers. How lucky for us to be people who built things and took our satisfactions from humming machines and running programs. We certainly wouldn't mind if the company went public and we all got fabulously rich. But the important thing was right in front of us. We had started with some scratchings on a whiteboard and built this: this operational program, this functional thing.

"And look," said the lead, demonstrating his handiwork, "You just click here, drag here, and click here—"

"And it *works*," I said.

"Yeah," he said, exhaling the word in a long breath of contentment, then standing back, exultant. "Yeah, it *works*."

[8]

I SAW BRIAN AGAIN.

It was my doing—I sought him out—though there wasn't any good reason for me to do it. We hadn't tried to contact each other. And I knew, through various intermediaries, that there was indeed a woman in his life. He and this woman had an odd, open relationship that had gone on for years, which I told myself was fine: I didn't want that sort of thing with Brian.

I sent him e-mail. Talks on the phone with Brian tended to be short and awkward, so e-mail was my preferred way of reaching him. But there was a network problem. My mail kept bouncing back at me, undelivered.

I was reduced to calling him. It was strange, but the words that had seemed properly cool in e-mail seemed too forward, made me feel too exposed, once Brian was breathing on the other end of the line. So I stupidly read him the e-mail message, verbatim, envelope included. "To: brian@exnet.com, From: ullman@neo.com, Subject: Saturday? Data: I thought it might be nice to see each other sometime when we didn't have to get up and go to work. How about Saturday? Quit."

Moment of dead air. Then: "Saturday? What's today? Monday? Tuesday?"

"Monday."

"I'm sure I'll have some time in the week. But I don't know about Saturday. I'll call you."

"Well, let me know by—"

"Yeah. I'll call you."

And we hung up.

But he didn't call. Not Tuesday or Wednesday or the next day. Not until noon on Saturday.

"I made other plans," I told him.

"I figured you would," he said.

It was impossible to know exactly what this statement meant. Was he more impressed with me for not having waited around? I think he saw me as fearlessly independent, not much caring whether I saw him or not. He probably would have been hugely disappointed if I had *not* gone off and made my own plans. This idea of me he had—of this free spirit, this mature woman who took what she wanted and dropped what she didn't—was wrong, but it wasn't his fault. He had seen me coming and going at the conference with my several elsewheres. I'd invited him out exactly this once. Otherwise, I hadn't exactly chased him. So it shouldn't have surprised me if he had a mistaken image of me: it was, after all, the exact image I'd wanted him to have.

"You know, Brian, we don't have to do this."

"No, no. Let's go out."

"When?"

Pause. "Saturday. Next Saturday."

"If you're—"

"Yeah. I won't blow it this time."

We went to a movie. He held my hand all through the show. Afterwards he waited for me outside the ladies' room. When I walked back out into the lobby, there was Brian leaning against a wall, with all the other boyfriends. I felt strangely pleased at the sight of him, at his high-schoolish, date-night good manners. It wasn't nostalgia—I had been a sullen, rebellious girl who drove off any boy who tried to get within a foot of me. No, it wasn't memory but the brief idea of some other life entirely. As he put his arm around me to make our way out, I had time to regret the morose young woman I'd been; to wish I had let a few more boys into my life to hold my hand at the movies and wait for me outside the ladies'.

What happened next was a mistake. Instead of just taking him home, I suggested a wine bar, one of my haunts. The place was sleek, the clientele dressy, the wine expensive. And there sat Brian, cowboy hat in lap. "Do they have peppermint tea?" he asked.

Maybe it was the stark reality of how mismatched we were. Maybe it was the political argument we stumbled into, where Brian showed off his cold, "moral-less" side. Maybe I had a subliminal understanding that if Brian and I reached each other again through whatever that physical thing was between us, I would only want more and more again, and that would be impossible. But when we finally did get back to my loft, and we were at last to get to the one thing that connected us, I drew back. Or my body did. One moment I was there with Brian, I was present in the all-there way that had drawn me back to him, and the next, I felt my body slide out from under me and disappear, like a fish swimming away into dark water.

"I think you're becoming real," I said.

"What does that mean?"

"Not just someone to sleep with."

I heard him sigh in the *uh-oh* sort of way men do. "Well, there are complications in my life I need to tell you about," he said. "But I'm too tired right now. I'll tell you all about it in the morning."

Whereupon he fell asleep.

I did not fall asleep. I knew instantly he'd misunderstood me. He probably thought the next thing I'd say would be a declaration of love, the desire for commitment, and so forth—all the messy business of relationship that usually brings on the *uh-oh* response. But I had explained myself badly. "Real" at that moment did not mean his realness so much as my own: I was suddenly tired of playing the sexual buccaneer.

I had a long night to consider why this was true. The pitched ceilings in my loft sent the reflections of headlights circling overhead, and I watched the lights fly around as I roamed through my past. I could no longer count the number of lovers I'd had. I could only remember the time when, with great surprise, I'd realized that the number of men and women had become about equal. After that, I'd let go of the ordinals, the list of names, in sequence, and what remained was a flickering serial memory of making love, and the constant amazement at how different it was with every single person.

It seemed to me I had taken lovers rather freely, without a lot of assurances or negotiations. I'd had three long-term relationships, marriages in essence. But I didn't need to marry everyone; not everyone had to fit into the whole of my life. I remembered one lover in particular, a man I would go off to visit whenever it occurred to me to see him. I never called first. I'd just show up and knock on his door. He could be there or not; he could be busy or not. If he was there and available, I'd stay. We would make love, go the movies, make love some more then sleep a little. In the morning, he'd make me strong coffee and rich scrambled eggs. We'd talk for a couple of hours. Then I'd leave. Between times, I never wondered what else he was doing. When we wanted to talk about our love interests, we did; when we didn't want to mention it, we didn't. This went on for years.

The deep friendliness of that old relationship—and its unnegotiated intimacy, most especially—became something of an icon for me. I wondered if I would ever find anything like it again. So here was my chance, yes? Why not with Brian? The traffic noise seemed too loud for that hour of the morning. I watched the reflections of headlights run up the walls, circle the ceiling, collide. *Why not with Brian?*

I conjured up the face of my old lover. I saw his body, his bed, the look of his kitchen, the way he brewed coffee by boiling the grounds. I remembered coming back from the movies then making popcorn and lazily watching another movie on the television while we talked. There it was: we talked to each other for hours. Our time together had a leisurely spaciousness in which he came to know me, and I him. All that knowing each other was what made possible our "open" relationship. Besides, we never called it that. We didn't intend anything; it was simply the unexpected place we came to with each other.

But Brian, I knew, started out with an idea: this will go only so far and no farther. We started out on a road that already had its dead end. What could be the point of such a relationship? It would be too much like a virtual reality, where things only *seemed* unpredictable and possible. Why bother with all the difficulty of another person if it could not go somewhere unexpected?

It seemed to me that my life was already too full of unconnected bits. Contracts that came and went. Companies founded and dissolved. Programs downloaded from the Internet, tried out, discarded. Intense moments with colleagues who then disappeared. Calls to names at 800 numbers who were usually gone if you asked for them again. I had stopped expecting much, I saw. It was too easy to live in these discrete, free-roaming capsules, a life like particles from an atom smasher, exploding into spectacular existence—for an instant—then gone.

I looked over at the sleeping Brian. And I felt sorry

for both of us. We weren't very brave. Surely we were missing something essential if our idea of other people was a program downloaded from the Internet.

Before I finally fell asleep, I remembered a conversation I'd had with an old friend, the one who recruited me into the communist party. We had both been pretty wild in our youth. I used to kid her that she'd slept with everybody—and she practically had. "How did we do it?" I asked her. "How did have so many lovers? And how did we go so blithely from one to the next?"

"You have it wrong," she said. "We weren't blithe. We suffered. We fell in love with all of them."

"Oh, right," I said. "I remember now."

In the morning, while we were still in bed, Brian told me about the woman he called his "main girlfriend." It all seemed reasonable enough. They had been together for four years. They didn't live together. They took other lovers. "I need a *lot* of psychic distance from her," he said.

I'd known about the girlfriend. But where did I fit in?

"And the others?" I asked. "Where are they?"

He looked at his feet. "They're more . . . *casual*," he said.

Casual. He might have said almost anything else—they're all different, they're important in particular ways, who knows what someone will be. But *casual.* . . . I felt myself float off and away from him. Whatever hold his sweet and unsweet sides had on me dissolved in that instant. It was like a sleeping foot coming back to life: first some pin sticks, then a little pain, then normal feeling again.

"You know, Brian, this isn't exactly my scene. I think we should stop sleeping with each other."

He seemed to be expecting this. "Okay. But I'd still like to see you."

How would we reach each other if we didn't have sex? But saying yes seemed to be the thing to do. "Sure. If it will be all right with you that we don't sleep together."

"Oh, yeah," he said with little laugh, "I have years of experience being celibate. I learned to control myself."

Months later, I learned just how many years Brian had spent controlling himself. How little experience he'd had with women, casual or not. How all his "polyamory" stuff was underway but still more notion than history. It was just as I'd suspected the first night I spent with him: he'd been with himself too long. Even his working life was mostly fantasy. His company never did set up an off-shore porn server. It did not control the secret paths of a Web click. There was no bank in the Caribbean. I have no doubt that one day some of Brian's schemes will become awfully real. But, just then, they were still the amoral dreamings of a young man who was too smart and too isolated for his own good.

Strangely, once it was clear that things between me and Brian were over, we relaxed. We lay in bed that morning and had our first friendly, truly personal conversation.

All the pillow talk we did not have before—where we came from, our families, our past lovers, the ones we liked the best—now came freely. I saw that I had not been wrong to have those poignant moments over Brian. Because under all his determination to be a pornographer, to have his "polyamorous" relationships, to be a cool cypherpunk, he really was trying to make contact as best he could. He just wasn't very good at making contact, which you really can't hold against someone, much as you'd like to.

Still, it took me a bit to get over the reasons I'd wanted to see Brian "sometime when we didn't have to get up and go to work." I'd had my delusions: I had visions of us lying on the sofa on Sunday morning reading the *Times*. I had this idea we would listen to Glenn Gould playing Bach's G Minor piano concerto. I imagined I would show him the way into this music, the slow movement's aching play of major against minor, the intense miracle of logic which, somehow, with all its precision and balance, still burst with passion. "Here is how I know God is a passionate engineer," I thought I might tell him.

But what could I have been thinking? Brian was a cryptographer, a specialist in hiding. He dreamed of creating a universe of anonymous transactions. Scrambled facts, anonymity—these are not the makings of someone who can attach to anyone. He wanted to hang out with his cypherpunks. He wanted to divide the world into the "main" and the "casual." Even before he could get near the sweet terrors of the possible, he tried to cordon himself off. He had a girlfriend from whom he needed "a lot of psychic distance."

I drove him to the train. In the car, he looked at me intently. "You know, I really *do* like you," he said.

"Of course you do," I said, patting his hand. "And I like you, too."

I let him off at his stop and got out to say goodbye. He hugged me, then held on for one last squeeze. "I'll call you in a couple of days," he said.

I thought it was sweet that he knew to say he really liked me, sweet that he knew to hug me goodbye, sweetest of all that he knew to say he would call. But as I watched him walk away — funny backside-twitchy walk under long hair and cowboy hat — I knew it would be best if we didn't call and we didn't try to see each other again.

And we didn't.

[9]

Inevitably, there is another contract. It begins, like the others, with a phone call. Someone I worked with recommended me. Am I available to design a new product? "Windows NT," murmurs the voice on the phone; "Internet," he says. But he doesn't really need to entice me. "Yes," I say, "I'm available." *Yes.*

This time, instead of going south to Silicon Valley, I drive east across the Bay Bridge. 9 AM: the road is clear and fast, and I'm across the bridge in no time. The freeway then heads south, through cities I've always known are there but have forgotten all about, then east again, toward Stockton. Just after the freeway takes a big turn inland, a line of semis merges from the left. They're like a wall moving toward me, fifty thousand pounds of roaring diesel momentum on a downhill ride to Central California. My car isn't as high as their wheels. It's not at all clear they see me. As I slip through them, moving left and left again as they move right, I remember why I bought this fast little car: when trouble comes, I have the choice of yielding or accelerating. I accelerate.

The company is in an office park built in a former pasture. A low haze still rests on the land, and for a moment I can see that this was ranch and farm not so long ago. There's still scrub; birds are busy in scraggly hedges. But in every direction are construction cranes and frames for new buildings just like the one in front of me. The birds won't be here for long.

I meet with the vice president of software development and the project manager. They tell me what they want from me: I'm to look at some software they're modifying and make suggestions; if "things work out," they want me to design some new software. I name a ridiculously high hourly rate. They agree. We all shake hands.

They take me into a conference room, where a computer and monitor are set up. Eight other people are already there: vice presidents, managers, programming leads. They all sit behind me. They are all there to watch me look at their software. It's an audition, I see. Twenty minutes ago, I didn't even know what this company did, but now ten people I've never met before will see if I have anything intelligent to say about software for payroll processing, electronic paycheck direct-deposits, wire-transfer filing of payroll taxes with the IRS—subjects I don't know much about.

"So the payroll is transmitted raw," I say.

"Yeah," says the lead, "Just a flat data stream—"

"And you do the calculations, the deposits—"

"—the deductions, taxes—"

"Then you turn around and transmit—"

"—the direct deposits, the taxes quarterly, the updated company files."

"Cool," I say.

"Yeah," says the lead.

Four hours go by. Somewhere in there, sandwiches appear and get eaten, cookies appear and disappear. Ten years ago, I would have been in a state of terror. But now the fear energizes me. I see down and down again toward the place where imagined money disappears into hardware and software. The world of money explodes. I feel like I'm taking off in a rocket.

"What is the primary work-flow paradigm?" I ask.

"We need you to help us define it," says the product manager.

"Are you committed to rewriting—?"

"Everything. From scratch."

Diet Cokes, coffee, cakes: two more hours go by.

"And do you have an idea for this Internet piece?"

"We thought it could be the same as the new client software."

"Oh, no. It can't be. There's a completely different expectation on the Web."

"What are you doing for the next year and a half?" asks the product manager.

Things have "worked out." I have passed the audition. I leave the meeting wired with thought waves, shake hands in a daze, hit the parking lot buzzed. I'm in a mental methedrine high that feels like exaltation.

But even as I drive home—T-bar roof open, wind

that feels like the rushing going on in my brain—I see how this phase will pass into the next. Soon enough, the computer will take me back to its own place, where the system and its logic take over. I'll start to worry about the payroll clerks using the software I design. I'll wonder what I'm doing helping the IRS collect taxes. It will bother me that so many entities—employer, software company, bank, IRS—know so much about the simple act of someone getting paid for labor delivered. I'll think about the strange path of a paycheck direct-deposit, how it goes from employer to bank, company to company, while the person being paid is just a blip, the recipient's account a temporary way station, as the money flows through the bank's hands into the hands of a borrower, then out again through the great engine of commerce.

And I'll have to muddle through without certainties. Without my father's belief that the machinery of capital, if you worked hard and long, was benign in the long run, so benign you could even own a piece of it. Without my generation's macho leftism, which made us think we could smash the machine and build a better one. Without Brian's cocksureness that he was smart enough to know all the machine's little secrets, and so control it.

But all that can wait. For now, I'm just going to enjoy where I am: at the beginning of a new contract, the rocket-takeoff learning curve, the exquisite terror of it, the straight-up ride against gravity into a trajectory not yet calculated. The next time I drive down to the company, a fog hangs lead-gray over the bay. It lingers over all the East

Bay cities. Then, where the freeway turns inland, the fog lifts and thins, and the sky turns a sheer glare-white. I race past the trucks, the hills shine deep green in the clear light, and, for the moment, I'm just where I'm supposed to be: driving a fast car to a place I don't know yet, where anything can happen.